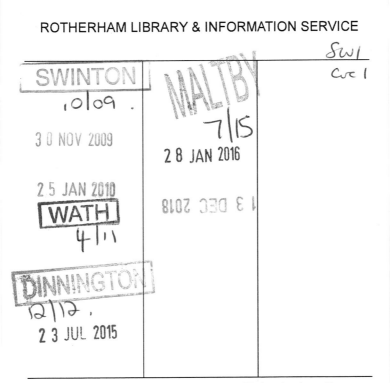
This book must be returned by the date specified at the time of issue as
the DATE DUE FOR RETURN.
The loan may be extended (personally, by post or telephone) for a
further period if the book is not required by another reader, by quoting
the above number / author / title.

Enquiries: 01709 336774

www.rotherham.gov.uk/libraries

Brian and Me

Brian and Me

An autobiography

Charles Collingwood

<small>WITH ALISON MALONEY</small>

Michael O'Mara Books

First published in Great Britain in 2009 by
Michael O'Mara Books Limited
9 Lion Yard
Tremadoc Road
London SW4 7NQ

A CIP catalogue record for this book is available from the British Library.

Papers used by Michael O'Mara Books Limited are natural, recyclable products
made from wood grown in sustainable forests. The manufacturing processes
conform to the environmental regulations of the country of origin.

ISBN: 978-1-84317-391-5

1 2 3 4 5 6 7 8 9 10

www.mombooks.com

Every effort has been made to trace the copyright holders of the images
in this book. Any errors or omissions that may have occurred
are inadvertent, and anyone with any copyright queries is invited to write
to the publishers, so that a full acknowledgement may be included in
subsequent editions of the work.

Designed and typeset by Design 23

Printed in the UK by CPI William Clowes, Beccles, NR34 7TL

To my complex diamond – with love.

Contents

Introduction

Who was it who said that to be a successful actor you need ten per cent talent and ninety per cent luck? No idea, but my luck changed when I met actress Judy Bennett, later to become my wife, and landed the role of Dave Escott in *The Archers*. That led to my being asked back to play Brian – and I shall never forget my first day in character.

It was 1975 and I was in my early thirties, with a few years as a jobbing (and sometimes not jobbing) actor behind me. It was wonderful to be coming back to *The Archers* and this time I knew it could turn into a major role. Brian was destined to be with Jennifer who was, after all, an Archer, so I was determined to get it right.

My first episode was at half past two in the afternoon so I arrived at the Pebble Mill studio early and thought I'd pop up to the canteen on the seventh floor for a bit of lunch before starting. As I walked into the lift I came face to face with the actor Jack Holloway, who for as long as I could remember had played the squire of Ambridge, Ralph Bellamy. I was delighted to see him again, because it was only a few weeks since I'd stopped playing Dave, and I said 'Jack, how are you?'

He looked at me with a face like thunder and grunted 'Terrible! Terrible!'

'Why?' I asked.

'I've just been written out of the ruddy programme!' he replied.

At that moment the lift got to the second floor, which housed the bar, and Jack stomped off out of the lift, to go and drown his sorrows at this frightful news. I carried on up to the canteen and got my tray of BBC food. The tradition in those days was for the cast to sit at one great big table and, as I approached them, the actors were generously calling out, 'Well done, Charles! Welcome back! Lovely, lovely to see you again, so pleased ...'

I interrupted them, to say, 'Thank you, but I just met Jack Holloway in the lift and he says that he's been written out of the programme.'

They looked at me in some surprise and somebody said, 'Yes, you've bought his farm.' You can imagine how thrilled Jack was to see me when I walked in the lift, can't you?

After digesting my lunch, along with this extraordinary piece of news, I went downstairs to sit outside Studio 3, BBC Pebble Mill, where I was to do my first scene as Brian, determined that it would be a runner. Just before I went in, a familiar voice hailed me and I was called over by Gwen Berryman, who had played Doris Archer from the first episode. When I joined the programme, Dan and Doris were one rung down from the King and Queen of England, so you stood to attention when either of them spoke. Gwen Berryman was sitting in her chair and I did indeed stand to attention.

'Charles, I want a word with you,' she began. 'There are two things you need to know about *The Archers*; the first one is that there are no stars in *The Archers*, *The Archers* is the star.'

I said, 'Yes, Miss Berryman,' noticing, however, that she had her name embroidered in the back of the chair she was sitting in. I let that go.

Then she said, 'The second thing is you're going to be asked to open fetes. Always charge the maximum!'

With those invaluable bits of information, I went into Studio 3 and played my first scene as Brian Aldridge.

Mind you, I've always known how to make an entrance, as one

story from my early days demonstrates.

After the war my father, like a lot of people who had been in the war, didn't have a job to go to and I think he had a tough time. Finally, he got the job he wanted – the one he knew he would do for twenty or thirty years. Even though I was a tiny little boy, no more than five, I could sense the excitement of my mother and father. I was an only child, we were a close-knit family and I could see how much more relaxed they were now that my father had got this job.

There I was, aged five, and my parents said, 'Now, tonight, Charles, we want you on your *very* best behaviour, because Mr Peto Bennett, the chairman of your father's new company, is actually coming for dinner in our house.' I was bathed and put in my pyjamas, so I smelt nice. Peto Bennett arrived and I was brought down by my mother to meet the man who was going to employ my father, possibly for the rest of his life. I was taken into the drawing room and my mother said, 'Mr Bennett, I'd like you to meet our son, Charles.'

He looked down and said, 'How do you do?'

I looked up and said, 'How do you do?' and he carried on talking to my father.

At which point, appalled, I tugged at his sleeve and said, 'Excuse me, haven't you noticed my eyes?'

Adults never think children can hear and I was one of those children about whom everybody said, 'Hasn't he got lovely eyes!' This was the first grown-up in my five years who hadn't said it, and I wasn't having that. I could see the colour draining from my father's face. Luckily, all was well and my father's career wasn't adversely affected.

In 2003, I was asked to take part in the Radio 4 show *That Reminds Me*, where guest speakers tell anecdotes about their lives. After the show, Peto Bennett's daughter wrote to me because she heard me tell that tale, and she said, 'It was so wonderful! I was at home and suddenly somebody's talking about my father who's been dead for twenty-five years.' It was lovely to hear that.

The radio show was perfect for me because I have always enjoyed a good story. A few years ago I was in Cheltenham at the Literary Festival and Stephen Pile, the reviewer from *The Times* came along to hear me speak. In the paper the next day, he wrote, 'Then Charles Collingwood spoke. He was relentlessly anecdotal.' And relentlessly anecdotal I intend to be throughout this book, so I hope it will raise a smile or two.

ONE

Beginnings

My grandfather Cuthbert Collingwood, whom I adored, had a wealth of anecdotes and was probably the person that got the stories going in my head as a little boy. He had the most wonderful friends who got up to all kinds of interesting adventures, and they used to get together at their London clubs to play cards until the early hours. There was one member of their group who would always do anything for a bet and, on one particular evening, they'd been playing poker. They'd had dinner, it was getting late and they said to this chap, 'We've all had a chat and we bet you a fiver each that you daren't – on the stroke of midnight – walk up the Mall to Buckingham Palace starkers.' Well, let's say there were nine of them, that's going to be forty-five quid which, in 1926, was a considerable sum of money. He thought about it for a second, and said, 'Done. I'll see you all at Trafalgar Square and we'll walk up together.' Off he went, and they all had another round of drinks, laughing all the while because they thought this was just brilliant.

At five to twelve they strolled down to Trafalgar Square to see this man make a complete twit of himself and get arrested. In the interim, however, he'd gone out and hired a taxi. 'Do you want to earn yourself a fiver?' he asked the driver. Well, in those days he could have driven to Liverpool in a taxi for a fiver.

'Yes,' said the driver.

'Right, take up the floorboards,' said the resourceful chap.

The driver duly did exactly that and at midnight this old boy got inside the taxi, took all his clothes off and, with his feet through the floorboards on the Mall and the cabby driving at three miles an hour, he walked all the way up to Buckingham Palace – and got his forty-five quid.

My grandfather Cuthbert, or Bertie as he was known, had many friends, one of whom was Gordon Selfridge, the owner of Selfridges. On one occasion Gordon said, 'Bertie, You're not going to believe this,' and he went on to tell the following extraordinary story. A female customer had gone to Swan and Edgar, the once-famous department store in Regent Street, and bought a powder compact. She put it in her bag and then got a taxi to Selfridges to continue her shopping. In the store, she saw the identical powder compact, so she picked her purchase out of her bag to check its price and found that, indeed, Selfridges' compact was a little more than the one in Swan and Edgar. So she put it back in her bag, thinking, 'Good, I got a good deal,' and carried on walking around.

As she left Selfridges, there was a hand on her shoulder and a security guard saying, 'Excuse me, madam, we saw you put that powder compact in your bag.'

'Well excuse *me*, young man, but I didn't get it here,' she said.

'Ha, ha,' said the security guard. 'I'm very sorry, but I'm afraid you did. Will you come with me?'

'Just a minute,' said the woman. 'I bought this in Swan and Edgar.' Now, in those days, it wasn't like today where you have receipts for everything and pay on credit card. It was cash and no receipt. So Selfridges started getting a bit heavy with her and she said, 'Look, I'm not having this. We will get a taxi, you and me, we'll go straight down to Swan and Edgar now and I will verify it.'

So, with a smile on his face, they went down to the other store, and found the salesman who said, 'Indeed, yes, an hour ago I sold this compact to this lady. She's right.'

At this point Selfridges have got egg on their face, so when she got back to the store she was showered with sincerest apologies, to which, very shrewdly, she told them, 'This is my name and address and I trust I'll get a letter from the store's owner.'

When she got home there was an enormous bunch of flowers outside her flat in Kensington and a little card saying, 'I cannot apologize enough for the appalling incident in my store. Please accept these flowers with my very best wishes. Please telephone my secretary because I would like to meet you personally to apologize.'

The lady rang his secretary there and then and was told, 'Gordon Selfridge would be happy to see you tomorrow morning at nine o'clock when the store opens.' The following day, she went to the fifth floor, where Gordon Selfridge had his suite, and rang the bell to his apartment.

He opened the door, took her inside and said, 'Madam, I can only apologize with all my heart. The only way I could really show you how sorry I am is to say that anything in the store you want is yours.'

And without pausing for breath she said, 'I'd like a grand piano.'

When Gordon Selfridge told my grandfather this story, he was laughing because this woman had obviously spent the entire night thinking what she wanted. 'What made me laugh especially,' he said, 'is that she didn't pause to think! She came straight out with "I'll have a grand piano."' Of course, she got her grand piano.

I often wonder why I ended up as an actor because there were no actors in my early life, but there were a lot of eccentrics, and my grandfather was one of them. He was the picture editor of *The Times of India*, which probably meant he didn't do a hand's turn and spent all day with his racehorses. Life in Calcutta was very comfortable, the family was pretty wealthy and lived in the most palatial colonial pile, with a host of servants.

In 1923, when it was time for my father, who was Grandpa's pride and joy, to go to school, he and my grandmother Grace packed up their things and came back to England by sea. On April Fool's Day, they were just off the Egyptian coast and my grandfather tipped the crew and told them, 'I want you to put out on the Tannoy that the ship is on fire.' They duly put out a plea, 'Everybody on deck, everybody on deck, fire on board.' In panic, the passengers appeared in their nightclothes and in their underclothes, to be greeted by my grandfather wielding a fire hose with which he soaked the lot of them, shouting 'April Fool, ha, ha!' How funny was that? Not!

The irony was that the following day the ship really did catch fire, off Port Said, and, of course, when the Tannoy announced, 'Fire, Everybody on deck!' the passengers said, 'Sod that! I'm staying in bed!' It took quite a bit of persuasion to get them out.

The fire took hold of the ship and they began to get the lifeboats out. The ship was going to go down. There happened to be some pilgrims on the ship and, according to my father, the main pilgrim went to the captain and said, 'If we sprinkle holy water on the flames they'll die down.' At this stage the captain was ready to try anything so he let him shake a few drops of holy water on the flames. 'And just for a few moments the flames did seem to abate,' my father told me. 'And we thought "Oh my God, it worked".'

However, the holy water wasn't as holy as they'd hoped, so up it went, the ship was lost, they were all put in lifeboats and saved. Unfortunately, all the possessions that they were bringing back in the hold of the ship are now at the bottom of the sea off Port Said, so the family pictures and heirlooms were lost.

After arriving in Britain, as far as I know, Grandpa never worked again. I have a feeling that he thought that if you had money, you just remained monied and you didn't have to earn anything more. When he came back he bought a house in Cheyne Walk in London – which my daughter Jane dearly wishes was still in the family – but he went on to lose all his money, so that didn't last very long. My grandparents then moved to Barnes and sent my father to St Paul's School in Hammersmith, but by the time I came along they were living in rented accommodation in Barons Court, with a lot of empty cupboards. Father told me that before the war Grandpa would charter a plane to fly to Liverpool to the Grand National and take all his friends, would probably lose a stack of money, and then fly back. Well, you don't live a lifestyle like that and stay in Cheyne Walk unless you've got shed loads of money coming in.

The grandfather I knew was an old man sitting in his leather chair in Barons Court and not really contributing an awful lot, while my grandmother, who loved him a great deal, fussed around. He'd had about three strokes by then and he was fairly immovable from this leather chair, but I remember that I would always kiss him on the forehead and say 'Hello, Grandpa,' and there would be a sort of a groan, then his shoulders would start heaving and he'd remember a joke. By the time he got to the punchline, all six foot two of him was standing up, belting out the final line, crying with laughter and I'd be on the floor doubled-up with laughter. Then he'd fall back in the chair and that'd be the last we'd get out of him, until I went to say goodbye. I would shake him by the hand, give him a kiss and there would always be a sweaty half-crown in his hand for me. I adored the old boy, but each visit would be followed by this terribly

confusing journey home where I'd be told to go to sleep in the
back of the car by my parents, and I could hear them talking in
low voices, saying 'bloody man' this and 'bloody man' that …
'hasn't got this' and 'he's wasted his money' and so on.

There was always something a bit show business about
Grandpa. He was a world champion bridge player and played
many times for Great Britain. It always annoyed my father that
he never wrote books about it. He could have written the
definitive book on defensive bridge playing, which would have
probably kept us in wine gums for the rest of our lives.

After he moved back from India, Grandpa lived his life in a
dinner jacket and was always in the clubs, wining and dining. It
can't have been much fun for my grandmother, although they
had a deep affection for each other. On his deathbed Grandpa
said to my father, 'Jack, we've been so lucky with our wives,'
which came as a bit of a shock to my mother because she wasn't
sure he thought much of her at all. My father always said that he
never came to their wedding, in 1942, which actually wasn't
true because I found their marriage certificate recently and
Grandpa had signed it. Under 'occupation' he had written,
'Independent', which is probably short for 'Of independent
means'. He should have written, 'Independent means fast
running out'!

It seems I come from a long line of lost fortunes. Indeed, in
1992, I discovered that I might well have been born to better
things if fate had been on my side. I was making a film called
Charles and Diana: A Palace Divided, in which I played Prince
Charles's private secretary. We were filming in Northumberland
and the Borders of Scotland, and we were staying in a little
village called Cornhill-on-Tweed, where we checked into a
hotel called the Collingwood Arms. All the other actors were no
doubt thinking, 'Christ, Charles is going to be impossible if

we're staying somewhere called the Collingwood Arms. He's bad enough as it is!'

Anyway, as I was signing the register the receptionist said, 'Are you related to Admiral Collingwood?' As you may know, he was second-in-command to Admiral Nelson at Trafalgar and is actually an ancestor of mine, so I said 'Yes'.

'Ah well,' she went on. 'There's a relation of yours lives in the village. His name is Eric Grounds.'

I'd never heard of him but she gave me his phone number and I called him.

'I'd like to come and see you,' I said.

'Do you drink red or white?' he replied, which I thought was a good start. Eric is related to Admiral Collingwood through marriage and is a particularly special guy, just one of those people who, when you are in his company, makes the world seem a better place. Safer, too, because he's enormous. Anyway, he studies genealogy and, as we chatted, he got out the family tree.

He then told me that the trouble with the Collingwood family is that every hundred years they shoot themselves in the foot; having thrown a double six to go up the ladder, they invariably go sliding down the snake! I'll never forget standing in his kitchen as he looked out at the Cheviot Hills, which were snowcapped at the time.

'Now, you see the Cheviot Hills over there, Charles?' said Eric. 'In about 1710 there was a battle and your lot had a fight against the other lot. Sadly your lot lost, otherwise you'd now be the Duke of Northumberland!'

And I remember going back to the Collingwood Arms thinking, 'I could have been the Duke of Northumberland. As it is I've got to go and learn my four lines for tomorrow morning's filming. Shucks ...'

We lived in the country, and as a child I was fascinated by the tube train that ran at the back of my grandparents' rented flat in Barons Court. I would sit in their garden and watch the line, and I thought that seeing tubes coming in and out of the tunnel was just the best thing. I remember my grandmother coming out and saying, 'Shall we go on the tube today?'

'Yes!' I said, very excitedly, so off we went to Knightsbridge. We were just going to go up and down the line, but then we were at Knightsbridge and she said, 'Well, shall we go into Harrods?' We went into Harrods and got in the lift which, in those days, had a proper attendant. You didn't push buttons; they told you which floor to go to and took you there. You could practically have tea in the lifts at Harrods back then, and I remember saying in a loud voice in this crowded lift, 'Granny, you've got your slippers on.' She wasn't too happy about that, and I don't think she took me to Harrods again.

Despite his deathbed endorsement, Grandpa disapproved of my father marrying my mother because she was five years older than him and because Grandpa didn't think she was posh enough. I think for 'posh' you could substitute 'rich'. He was always a bit of a freeloader and I think he wanted my father to marry somebody with vast estates and plenty of money so *he* could be kept, let alone my father. It wasn't to be, though, because my mother came from a large family and, although her father worked as a civil servant in the Foreign Office, he didn't have an enormous amount of money. It's odd too that Grandpa disapproved of my mother being five years older than my father. Years later, we found out that my grandfather had been married before he met Grace – to a woman ten years older than him. What a hypocrite!

My mother's side were comfortable, middle-class Londoners and her ancestors included William Mason, who was a pretty successful watercolourist. He was a good friend of Dickens, and his claim to fame is that in 1843 he was commissioned to colour the first Christmas card. It was designed by John Calcott Horsley, RA, and printed in black and white, then each copy was painstakingly coloured by Mason.

After meeting in London during the war, my parents – Henry Ernest Collingwood (always called Jack) and Evelyn Mary Atherton (always known as Molly) – were married in 1942 at St Mary Abbots, High Street, Kensington.

At the time of their marriage my father was in the RAF. Father was very good-looking and one day, when he was in uniform and sitting with my mother on the tube, he made a classic remark.

'Do you see all those people sitting over there?' he said.

'Yes,' said my mother.

'Do you know what they're all thinking?'

'No. What?'

'They're all thinking how come that devastatingly good-looking man is married to that rather plain woman.'

We Collingwoods have a knack for a turn of phrase that isn't always acceptable!

I imagine my mother laughed. They laughed a lot together. He wasn't a cruel man but he had been pampered by his parents and my grandmother's sister, Lena, who lived with them, and he was used to getting his own way. In many ways I think he married a mother figure. My mother was five years older and there was a certain amount of truth in what he said; she wasn't a beautiful-looking woman – although she was attractive and he always said she had the best legs – but she was a wonderful mother, to me and my father.

My father joined the RAF because he wanted to be a fighter pilot. The trouble was, he couldn't land planes. He buckled them instead. Every time he landed there was a terrible bump and the wheels bent a bit, and after a few times the powers that be decided he was costing the nation a fortune, so they sent him and my mother to Canada. He became an Instructor Officer working, one assumes, on the old adage that those who can, do and those who can't, teach. This turned out to be a very good thing, because there was damn all to do in Canada so they went to bed and made me.

I made my debut on 30 May 1943, in Saint Stephen, New Brunswick. By this time my father was in Bomber Command and was stationed at Penfield Ridge, New Brunswick. We stayed in Canada until the middle of 1944 and then came back to Britain, so my parents had a pretty easy war compared to most.

Officers and their wives were not allowed to travel on the same boat, so when they arrived in New York my father sailed on a troop ship, leaving my mother and me waiting for another boat. My mother took me to the foot of the Empire State Building, just so that in years to come she could say that we had both seen it.

As she stood looking up at the magnificent building an American woman in a mink coat asked, 'Is that your little baby?'

'Yes, it is,' replied my mother.

'Are you British?' asked the lady.

'I am,' answered my mother.

'Are you on your way back to England?'

Mindful of the wartime slogan, 'Be like Dad. Keep Mum!' Mother just said, 'Shortly, yes.'

'Listen,' said the lady, taking off her mink coat and wrapping me in it. 'I don't want you going home saying your little boy hasn't been to the top of the Empire State Building. I'll wait for you down here, you take him up to the top.'

So, wrapped in this woman's mink coat my mother took me, aged fourteen months, and all snug and warm, to the very top of the Empire State Building. She had a good look round, took me down again and handed this lady back her mink coat.

The journey home took over a week, and they had to have a Navy convoy zipping up and down because of the German U-boats. It can't have been easy for a young mum, but my mother was one of those people who just got on with things. I mean she wasn't 'jolly hockey sticks', she was very feminine, but she was intelligent, she was bright.

At the end of the war, we moved into a little cottage called Hart's Leap Lodge, in Sandhurst, near Camberley in Surrey.

My mother always used to say the secret of a good marriage is where the wife is slightly more intelligent than the man, but the man doesn't realize it, and that certainly applied to my mother and father. They were always seemingly happy and I don't remember any rows. It may be that my mother wouldn't allow them. She was one of those warm and wonderful mothers for whom I'd have had requests played for on the radio as the best mother in the world, if I'd been that sort of person. My mother was very loving to me and to my friends and was much the best maker of cheese-and-tomato sandwiches the world has ever known!

My father was a good sportsman, so he'd always play football and cricket with me and my friends, and always had time for us. He was a wonderful father because he was a boy at heart himself and that's something I think I've inherited from him. We didn't have much money but as a child it was always my house that my friends wanted to come and play in, although their parents were better off than we were. I was the only one in our circle who didn't have a live-in nanny, I just had my mother and father and a few aunts, but the atmosphere was always great in our house.

My mother was very tolerant of my father, who liked a drink and liked to party. He had some very eccentric friends as well. One such was a racing driver called Duncan Hamilton, with whom he'd go drinking. Duncan used to race at Brooklands and on one occasion he rang my father.

'Let's go out drinking,' he said. 'Let's go on a pub crawl.'

My father agreed and half an hour later Duncan turned up in an ambulance.

'For God's sake!' said my father. 'I'm not going on a pub crawl in an ambulance! Go back and get a proper car.' So away he went, and twenty minutes later he came back with a fire engine! By then my father was dying for a drink, so he threw in the towel and off they went pub-crawling in a fire engine.

It was just after the end of the war, they were all still young, damn lucky and grateful to be alive, so there was a spirit of carnival quite a lot of the time. Meanwhile, I was just growing up in my own happy little world.

Two

Schooldays

The day my father dropped me off at Sherborne School for the first time, aged thirteen, he shook my hand.

'Now, don't worry, old boy,' he said. 'You don't have to do any work, because I know everybody!' And with that he got in his car and drove off.

My unremarkable academic career began at a little pre-prep school called Waverley, where I quickly disgraced myself. We called it Miss Greenup's because the headmistress was called Miss Greenup. She was a fearsome woman, who was probably only five feet two, but she appeared to be seven feet tall to me. When we arrived in the morning in our little green caps we all had to file past her window, a sash window, which was open in the summer. She would sit there as we took off our caps and said, 'Good morning, Miss Greenup.'

I started at the age of four and by the time I was five I was travelling on the bus and walking up the road to Waverley alone. That's what life was like then and it was fine, although you couldn't do that now.

One day when I was six and beginning to read and write and show an interest in things, I was on the bus and the window was all steamed up so, of course, I wrote in the steam. Later that morning I was sent for by Miss Greenup. In her study she towered over me and said, 'Charles, what was the word you wrote in the window of the bus?' (The bus driver had reported me – a six year old – for writing on the window – bastard!)

I looked up nervously and stammered, 'Bosom.'

'What!' said Miss Greenup.

'Bosom.'

'You wrote *what?*' Her voice was getting louder by the moment.

'Bosom.'

'*Bosom?*' she boomed, in her best Lady Bracknell voice. 'You wrote bosom in the …' she spluttered. I was terrified. 'You will stay in and you will *not* go out for break.'

So I was made to stay in, probably to write out, 'I must not write bosom in the window,' a hundred times. What I do remember was one teacher after another coming in and asking, 'Charles, why aren't you out in the playground?' and having to answer, 'Because I wrote bosom in the window of the bus.' And I remember they all ran out then. Looking back on it, they must have been saying to one another, 'Go on, ask him. Ask him what he wrote on the window!' and giggling furiously because I wrote 'bosom'. Good for them!

I'm not surprised at my choice of words because I've had a lifelong interest in breasts ever since – and that's not the only time it got me into trouble. In 1987, *The Archers* took over the Watermill Theatre in Newbury and we turned the whole place into Ambridge. It was a huge hit and we had a month in paradise. It was such a success, in fact, that we transferred up to London, where we tried to repeat the experience in a four-acre marquee in Battersea Park. Huge fun, but Ambridge in Battersea Park, under canvas, was not a success.

In one of the scenes, Brian had to come on, rush up to Eddie Grundy and say, 'And another thing, Eddie, what happened to those ten missing bullocks?' That was the line. I'd done it all the way through Newbury; I'd now done it for two weeks in Battersea Park. So for six weeks running I'd come on and said,

'And another thing, Eddie, what happened to those ten missing bullocks?'

On one particular night, I ran on stage and I said, 'And another thing, Eddie, what happened to those seven missing bosoms?' Now, dear reader, bosoms I can understand – but why seven? Perhaps only a psychiatrist could answer that.

Back in my schooldays, my first foray into the world of acting ended badly, I'm afraid. I was playing one of the wise men in the Nativity play at Miss Greenup's and I told my parents I had a terrible pain in my tummy. Of course, they took me to the doctor, there was a lot of whispering and I was told I had to go into hospital to have my appendix out.

'When?' I enquired.

'Straight away, I'm afraid,' they answered.

'I can't do that! I'm in the Nativity play, I'm one of the wise men!' I said in outraged tones.

'I'm sorry about that, Charles ...' So, howling, I was carted off to this little cottage hospital in Yateley to have my appendix out. I remember being told by the person who was going to put me to sleep that I had to be very brave, that they were going to put a mask over my face and I had to blow into it and then suck in.

'It's like a balloon really,' he said. 'And if you're a very good boy you can have a balloon afterwards.'

They clamped this mask onto me – it didn't smell very nice, I have to say – but it put me to sleep. I woke up feeling pretty groggy having had my appendix out and to my surprise there were balloons tied all around my bed. About three days before Christmas, when I was sitting up and still a little sore, the Mayor of Camberley came round, dressed in his chains, for a sort of 'royal' hospital visit. He and his wife came to my bed, took one look at my angelic face, and said, 'Would you sing to us?' I imagine they were expecting 'Away in a Manger' or 'While

Shepherds Watched', but I stood up, started clicking my fingers and sang, 'You are my sunshine, my only sunshine ...' This rather startled the Mayor and his entourage, but I think that it was an early glimpse of the show business instinct creeping in.

The next day the medical team gathered at my bedside. I was desperate to go home for Christmas and I was OK, just a bit stitched up, a bit sore. There was a lot of whispering and, to my joy, I was told I could go home on Christmas Eve, but it would be straight to bed. So I happily returned home.

'Come on, Charles,' said my mother. 'You've got to do as you're told. Go straight up to your room and go to bed.'

I opened my bedroom door and I couldn't believe my eyes. There was a proper Christmas tree on the bedside table, all lit up and I thought 'Wow!' I got into bed, had a little sleep and when I woke up it was dark and I could hear men's voices downstairs. Then I heard my father say, 'If you'd like to come this way, it's up here.' My door opened and Father Christmas walked into my bedroom! I'd only just got out of hospital that morning and I'd got my own tree, now here was Father Christmas, who came and sat on my bed and talked to me about my appendix. He said I was a brave boy (which of course I was!) and asked me what did I want for Christmas? I can't remember what I asked for but he said, 'If you're a good boy I'm sure these things might happen,' then he shook me by the hand, said 'Have a lovely Christmas, Charles' and was gone. I heard my father saying, 'Thank you, Father Christmas, for sparing the time on such a busy day.' Magic!

Of course, my dear father had gone to the local department store in Camberley and paid the store Santa a fiver to come and sit on my bed. That was the sort of parents I had.

In later life, my father became rather a pathetic figure. He had a nervous breakdown in his fifties, partly because he'd never been made to face up to life's challenges. Always sheltered and protected from decision-making, he'd been cosseted by his parents and spoilt by my mother, so he was never taught how to take responsibility and I believe that's why he cracked in the end. It was terribly sad.

But those early memories of my perfect childhood made me realize how special my parents were. People would say, 'Your dad was so difficult when he got older', but I thought, 'No, it is my turn to look after him, be patient and understanding and be there for my mother.' It wasn't always easy.

A year or two before he died, my father needed a hernia operation. Couldn't be simpler: in on Tuesday, out on Thursday. He was crabby when Mother and I visited on the Wednesday after the op. He scorned the grapes and hardly seemed to acknowledge the news that I'd be collecting him the following day.

At nine o'clock that evening, back at my parents' home, the phone rang and the hospital night sister informed us that Mr Collingwood was dressed, packed and had ordered a taxi home. My mother and I looked at each other in disbelief – he had discharged himself. Sure enough, half an hour later he arrived home, ordering me to pay the taxi and get him a large whisky and soda.

Luckily, their dear, understanding GP had come at once to support us, and told my father, 'Go to bed – and NO WHISKY!' He'd only just had the operation and the anaesthetic, for goodness' sake.

In the morning he woke in a certain amount of discomfort and called out that he wanted me to help him into his dressing gown and into the drawing room. And there he sat, like an old colonial, with a very self-satisfied look on his face.

'Father,' I started. 'You must *never* behave like that again.

How dare you discharge yourself? I was going to fetch you this morning.'

He looked at me, 'The man in the next bed was a homo!'

'Father,' I said, looking at the pathetic figure in front of me. 'Danny La Rue at his *randiest* wouldn't have fancied you!'

'I wasn't taking the risk,' was his reply.

As I said, it wasn't always easy. But I always say to people that if they love their parents, try to be understanding if they start getting a bit crabby, because they are not going to be around much longer. You mustn't undo all the goodness of forty or fifty years just because they are difficult when they get older.

My father died on 1 January 1995 and, four years later, in May 1999, my mother died in my arms at the age of eighty-nine. It was the greatest privilege of my life, and I had the most remarkable experience, almost beyond description. As I sat with her, I know I saw her spirit leave her body.

In September 1951, at the age of eight, I was sent to a little prep school called St Neot's in Eversley, Hampshire. Run by a lovely eccentric old clergyman called the Reverend Aubrey Hooper, it was a huge place, set in seventy acres of land and woodlands, and had an outdoor swimming pool. On my first night, about ten of us little new boys sat in Matron's room, all in our new pyjamas and new dressing gowns and trying not to cry. Matron looked more like a man than a woman, but she was kind and she was giving us cocoa before we went to bed, probably reading us a story in a rather deep voice. In came the headmaster.

'OK boys,' he said. 'Come on, it's time for you to go to your dormitory now.' We went into the corridor, and he told us, 'Now, we're all mice. I'm the chief mouse and you're the little mice. Follow me and do as I do.' Off he went, prancing down this long corridor, off which all the dormitories ran. We tiptoed behind, prancing like him, with our little hands like mouse paws, until we got to the final corner by our dormitory.

'Right, stay there,' he commanded. 'Count up to ten and then come into your dormitory, which is through that door.' So we counted up to ten, opened the dormitory door and the headmaster of my prep school, the old clergyman, was in my bed with all the sheets and the blankets pulled up to his chin. We just fell about laughing. Then he got out of bed, said 'Goodnight boys, sleep well' and turned the light out.

Over and above his role as a clergyman and headmaster, he was a father with four children of his own, and he knew he needed to take our minds off missing our mums and dads. It was an inspired thing to do, but can you imagine anyone doing that now, with all the political correctness and worries about paedophilia? He was simply a dear old dad who thought, 'I'll stop them crying on their first night'. Mind you, I think we cried like hell on the second night!

Before I went to prep school I had been in a fir cone fight with some friends back at Miss Greenup's. We had these lovely brown open fir cones and we chucked them at each other and if one of them hit you, you were dead. I was always quite good at sport and I was excellent at throwing, so I thought 'I'm going to introduce this game when I get to my new school.' How silly was I? I'd only been there two days and I found the thirteen-year-olds didn't pick the ripe brown ones – they went for the green ones. They were like stones winging through your hair and if you weren't careful, you'd lose an eye. We soon learned to duck.

All in all I didn't mind my prep school. There was a little bit of bullying, but there were individual bullies rather than institutionalized bullying. In the second term, the new boys had a special day, which was called a bashing-up day. That was pretty horrid because nobody spoke to you, and you weren't passed the food at the table and then everywhere you went you were given a bash and a smack.

On my bashing-up day I actually hit one of the senior boys back. He was about twelve and when he hit me it was quite painful, so I lashed out and got him absolutely smack in his face, right in the eye. He had such an impressive shiner, I was really rather pleased with myself.

The worst thing about prep school was the food, which was disgusting. It was just after the war so we had such delicacies as marrow jam, and slugs seemed to come with everything. Initially, sweets were still rationed but that stopped a year or so after I arrived. There were about six day boys in the school and what little money we could squirrel back into our pockets without being caught, we gave to the day boys to go and buy sweets.

Actually I was beaten by the old clergyman in the first term I was there, for going round by the swimming pool, which was out of bounds (quite right because it was bloody dangerous). It was towards the end of the term and the Reverend called me into his study.

'Charles, you know it's forbidden to go round by the pool,' he said. 'I'm going to beat you so you'll never go again. Bend over. Put your head on that chair.' And I remember thinking, even aged eight, that it was rather ironic that I should be lowering my head onto the parish magazine as I heard the swish of the cane above me!

In those days at schools you got beaten for almost anything, but I only got it once at St Neot's (though there were plenty more beatings in my latter years at Sherborne). It didn't hurt very much, and my father thought it was hilarious when I told him. Parents went along with things like that then. Those were just the rules.

In the second term, when my parents dropped me off at school I cried like hell. We were supposed to go into the library, which was just off the main entrance, and I was grabbing onto my parents and pleading with them not to go. My parents were in a terrible state and my mother was saying, 'How can we leave our little boy?' Anyway eventually they did leave me, in floods of tears … and halfway down the drive they discovered I'd left my cap in the back of the car. They turned round and came back and my father brought the cap inside. When he looked through the crack in the door, I was rocking with laughter. In the space of minutes it was all fine, and to this day I think an awful lot of boys and girls cry to upset their parents, not because they're particularly unhappy. That was certainly the case with me and I don't think I ever cried again when they left me.

Boarding school didn't bother me. I understand that some people hated it, but I didn't. I was an only child at home, with no brothers and sisters, so getting to school became a chance to be with my mates. And because of the sort of background I came from, I thought boarding was the norm. I was good at cricket and football, which stood me in good stead, and I ended up as Head Boy at the school.

We played cricket against Ludgrove, which was frightfully smart and a serious feeder school for Eton and Harrow. The captain of cricket at Ludgrove was a boy called Mike Griffith, who went on to captain Sussex. On the day we played them, we got off the coach at Ludgrove, shook hands like adults then walked down this immaculate path to the cricket field. To our far left there was another immaculate path so I asked what was the significance of these mown paths?

'Well, except on match days,' Mike told me. 'The one we're walking on today is for the exclusive use of boys who are going to Eton.'

What about the other immaculate path?' I asked.

'That's for the exclusive use of boys going to Harrow.'

'What about the unmown path in the middle?'

'That's for boys going to other schools!!'

To start with I was down for Eton, but my father found the fees at my prep school hard enough to manage, let alone the fees at Eton, with all the hidden extras. It was a serious worry to him, so he went to see my headmaster and asked, 'What do you suggest?' The old boy had been to Sherborne, in Dorset, and he suggested I follow suit. My father had always wanted me to go to a school that was part of a town, not up a long four-mile drive, because he was always wary of schools up long drives: if they're good, they're good, but if they're bad, nobody knows. The nice thing about Sherborne (and Eton is the same) is that you know you're in the town. You can go to the post office, or the bank or to Boots and you're with other people.

Sherborne is a beautiful market town in Dorset. Surprisingly, this sleepy little farming town has produced a number of successful performers, including Jon Pertwee, Lance Percival, Jeremy Irons, *Dad's Army* star John Le Mesurier and Hugh Bonneville – not to mention Chris Martin of Coldplay.

Of course, it is also the Alma Mater of Brian Aldridge and his stepson, Adam, so it has had frequent mentions on *The Archers*. On one occasion, when the Aldridges had a rather flighty au pair called Eva, Jennifer was outraged by the avid courting by one of the boys from the village and had the line, 'Do you know he was trying to climb up the outside of the house and get into Eva's bedroom last night! Disgraceful, isn't it?'

Brian, however, laughed the whole thing off and said, 'Oh, come on. We were always doing things like that when I was at Sherborne.' The day after the broadcast, the producer at the time, William Smethurst, was in his office and the phone rang.

It was the furious headmaster of Sherborne School.

'I think it's disgraceful, suggesting our boys climb into girls' bedrooms,' he said.

'I think, headmaster,' said William, 'it was a bit tongue in cheek. There was a lot of humour there.'

'Yes, but nonetheless, it's not something that should be ...'

William interrupted and played his ace card. 'Headmaster,' he said. 'I take your point, but may I just say you are the only leading independent public school we're giving free publicity to about four times a week. But if you'd rather we never mentioned it on the programme, then we'll stop it at once.'

'Oh no, no, no, no, no,' spluttered the headmaster. Game, set and match to William.

Anyway, in 1957, with my father's classic comment ringing in my ears, I embarked on my career at Sherborne School. The school occupies the town and, from the house where I boarded, it took me ten minutes to cycle to the centre. Every boy in the school had a bicycle because it was on the school list, along with the white shirts, stiff collars and the obligatory suits and ties. We cycled to the playing fields and to town, although we could walk to school from my house. There were six or seven houses dotted round the town and they had anything between sixty and eighty boys in them, all boarding. The housemaster and his family lived in private quarters while the boarders slept in dorms.

I liked Sherborne, although true to my father's advice, I didn't do much work. In fact, I seemed to spend most of my time in a class called The Remove, which I think is the lowest stage before being removed.

In one of my last reports, my housemaster said, 'Sadly we think O level is Charles's academic ceiling.' It was. This was brought to my parent's attention when I was sixteen and the headmaster called my parents in.

'Mr and Mrs Collingwood,' he said. 'You will understand there are six hundred boys in this school and I can't know them all particularly well, but I do feel I know Charles as though he was my son.' They were thrilled, of course. Until he added, 'But for all the wrong reasons ...' I didn't care. I wanted to be in show business and be a stand-up comedian.

When I was small, I didn't find things funny but by the time I was Sherborne I thought *everything* was funny. I noticed as a very young boy that we humans have a habit of laughing after we say something, even if it's not a joke. My father would say things like 'Molly, can I get you a glass of sherry?' and then laugh. I'd try to analyse it – why is that funny? Why is 'Can I get you a glass of sherry?' funny? But it's just a thing that humans do. Even at that early age I was interested in humour, and I always loved variety acts. I'd love to have been a stand-up comedian, but coming from my background it was hard enough being an actor, let alone saying to my father 'I want to be a stand-up comic.' He would have gone potty, and I don't think I'm nearly brave enough or funny enough.

At prep school I used write variety shows and plays – I always played the lead, of course – and they used to make Matron laugh. She always laughed at my jokes. Whether the rest of the school thought it was funny I'll never know. But by the time I reached Sherborne I was also quite keen on playing the piano, and I was into swing.

My lovely housemaster at Sherborne was a man called Frank King, who was a Cambridge cricket blue, short back and sides, and called us all 'chaps'. He had a sweet wife, and I was very fond of them both. However, he didn't approve of this sort of music at all and, during my four years at Sherborne, we played an interesting cat-and-mouse game together. The dining hall had a piano in it, so I would gather some housemates around me and entertain them by playing swing and singing 'Somebody Stole my Gal' or something similar. There was a door through to the private side where the housemaster and his family lived, and beyond that, down three steps, was his study. Both doors – his study and the dining room – had rattling handles, and when I played the piano I could hear him coming because he would always rattle them, giving me a chance to get out of the dining room before he got there. He was a very fair man but if he caught me I was beaten, simple as that. He only caught me twice in the four years.

To my annoyance, Frank King insisted on me having my hair cut all the time. Journalist Nigel Dempster was a contemporary of mine, and he always swaggered around Sherborne with his umbrella more tightly furled and his boater at a more rakish angle than the rest of us, with his hair slightly down on the top of his collar. In 1958, that was terribly smart and I wanted to be like that. But Frank used to say, 'Two shillings for you, my boy' because that's what it cost to have your hair cut at the barbers' in the town. In a way I didn't mind because by then I was smoking. I used to go into the paper shop and buy my cigarettes then arrive at the barbers' at one minute to six, just before closing time. The barber would put a closed sign on the door so I could sit inside and have two or three cigarettes and a cup of tea while he worked away.

Mind you, I didn't like what I walked out with, because I walked out with no bloody hair. Looking at me now it seems pathetic that I should have cared so much about my hair ... but, oh, the vanity of youth.

After I left school I went back in the summer holidays to play in a cricket festival with the old boys, and we stayed in the house with my housemaster and his wife.

'Charles, two things I want to tell you,' said Frank's wife Maggie at breakfast one morning. 'Firstly, you know all the time you were here at Sherborne, Frank was always making you have your hair cut?'

'Yes I do,' I muttered through gritted teeth.

'Well, dear, I want you to know I was always on your side, I was always saying to Frank, "Why don't you leave him alone? Why don't you grow your hair longer like Charles does? It's so nice".'

So I thought, 'Oh really – charming! I'll have another piece of toast.' As I helped myself to more toast she said, 'And there's another thing. You know the piano playing and how Frank used to rattle the door handle?'

'*Do* I remember that? Of course I do,' I said.

'Well I want you to know that on a number of occasions, before he rattled the door handles, we used to be dancing on the private side together.'

Wasn't that camp? There's such an old-fashioned sense of honour about it all. When I got my first big contract presenting a children's TV series, I wrote to Frank saying, 'I know I was probably a bit of a waste of space, but I'd be jolly grateful if you watched me on the telly.'

He wrote me the most wonderful four-page letter back, so uplifting and full of encouragement. Some years later, by which time he and Maggie had retired to a little house in Sherborne, Judy and I used to drop in to see them if we were going to the West Country. When he died Frank's son, Martin, asked me if I would speak at his memorial service in the school chapel.

'Are you sure you've got the right person?' I said. 'There are some very distinguished boys from my house who've done a lot better than me.'

But he said the nicest thing. 'Do you realize that until the day he died, my father had a photograph of you on his desk because he felt that, despite your differences, he'd cracked it with you.' I thought that was lovely.

'Your parents *liked* me?' I said, surprised by this revelation. 'I never did a hand's turn.'

'They used to say you were such fun,' he told me. As a boy you don't know that, but looking back on it gives me great warmth.

The wonderful thing about Frank King was that he was consistent. He never changed, he would always say good morning to you, he would always smile; he didn't cut you dead one day and be nice to you the next. He was absolutely dependable and you knew where you were with him, which is important when you're a boy, particularly if you're a bit of a rebel as I was.

In the summer we used to have early-morning school so that we could play cricket in the afternoon. We'd get up at quarter to seven and have a lesson before breakfast, then chapel at quarter to nine, and lessons started again at nine o'clock. There was a master called Micky Walford. The only problem with Micky was that all the boys, even me, felt they were slightly cleverer than he was, but he was a truly great games player. He had captained Great Britain at hockey, played cricket for Somerset, he got a half-blue at squash, he was a very good golfer and would have played rugger for England but for the war. We games players absolutely loved Micky, he was fantastic, and he always called me Charlie rather than Collingwood. Sadly, I was also in Micky's class for maths. He would write something on the board, stare at it and say, 'Does anyone know how to work this out?'

On one early-morning school session, when I was about sixteen, I walked up from my house into Micky's classroom. He stared at me.

'Charlie,' he said. 'What have you got on your feet?'

'Do you know, I honestly don't know, I've only just got out of bed, sir,' I replied. Then I looked down and exclaimed, 'Oh, they're my slippers.'

'Slippers! What are you wearing your slippers for?' he asked.

'Come on, it's barely light, sir, just got my slippers ...'

'Charlie, you're an inferior Teddy Boy,' he said. 'Come out here, I'm going to beat you.'

So at twenty past seven in the morning he got out his cane and gave me three whacks on the bottom.

When he'd finished I said, 'Excuse me sir, I object.'

'What do you mean you object?' he said, thinking I was going a bit far.

'I object to the word inferior!'

I wasn't a model schoolboy and neither was I a model soldier. In 1958, only thirteen years after the end of the Second World War, the Combined Cadet Force (CCF), or School Corps, was very strong in the Independent sector, so we were compelled to dress up as soldiers at least once a week and parade around with ancient rifles, pull them through, spit and polish our boots and blanco our spats. Oh, how I detested it! Over the years, I've played any number of officers in the services and, of course, I admire the military enormously, but it wasn't for me.

Every year at Sherborne we had the General's inspection, which was held on the Upper cricket ground, and row upon row of boys lined up in their platoons, in shiny boots, with newly cropped hair, badges polished and rifles at the ready. Such was my inability to pass any of the tests which aided promotion that, by my last summer term, when I was seventeen, I was still an ordinary private in the CCF. Not only that, but the other privates were all fourteen-year-olds, so when the General came along the line I stood out like a sore thumb because I was a lot taller and sported a fair amount of five o'clock shadow. The General seemed intrigued as he reached me and stopped to chat. At his side was the headmaster, Robert Powell, who was very dapper in dark blue bowler hat with furled umbrella, and Major Michael Earls-Davis who ran the CCF and had been a distinguished soldier in the Irish Guards. The General asked my name and, instinctively, I went into actor mode.

'Collingwood, sir,' I barked.

'And what are you going to do when you leave school?' he asked.

Without a moment's thought I shot back at him, 'I'm going in the army, sir,' at which point the headmaster and Major Earls-Davis had to turn away because, even on this rather formal occasion, they found that fairly amusing.

To my horror the General looked at me and said, 'Good, good. We need chaps like you,' and then carried on down the line. It took all my self-control not to call him back and say, 'No, you don't. What are you talking about? You don't need anybody like me in the army!' Looking back now, I know I was taking the mickey – but perhaps he was too!

I shared a study with Richard Eyre, who became *Sir* Richard Eyre the distinguished theatre director who used to run the National Theatre. I wish I'd known then, I'd have probably been nicer to him! Actually, when Paddy Greene, who plays Jill Archer, had her seventieth birthday, I rang Richard up and we met at the Groucho Club, because I wanted him to sign a copy of his recently published book as a gift for Paddy. We sat in a room with a bottle of wine and went over old times, and I congratulated him on his wonderful career.

'Little did I know that when we were young boys at school together you'd have such a distinguished career in the theatre,' I said, then I asked, 'Do you know what I do?'

'Charles,' he said. 'I know everything about you. I know all about Judy. I mean it's *unhealthy* how much I know about you. Judi Dench and I ring each other up every Sunday to talk about it so, fear not, I am your biggest fan.' That was wonderful to hear. I mean, Judi Dench!

A few years later, Judy and I went to see Judi Dench in a play in the West End and plucked up courage to go to the stage door and ask, 'Could we see Judi Dench, please?'

The stage doorkeeper asked who was calling and then rang the dressing room. In a distinctly surly voice he said, 'Charles Collingwood and Judy Bennett from *The Archers*. Certainly, certainly.' When he came off the phone his voice had a very different tone. 'If you go up to the second floor and wait outside for a minute, Judi Dench would be delighted to see you.'

So we arrived on the second floor and moments later the door was flung open.

'How wonderful,' said Judi Dench. 'I'm thrilled – come in.' She thrust a glass of champagne in our hands, saying, 'This is the most wonderful thing, I can't believe you're standing here in the dressing room.' Judy and I were open-mouthed. We chatted for a moment, drank our champagne and met some of the other guests and then we thought it was time we left, so we made our farewells. 'I can't believe you're in here,' said Judi. 'I can't wait to tell all my friends that I had Brian and Shula in my dressing room.'

'You can be damn sure I can't wait to tell all my friends where we were either,' said I.

My best friend at Sherborne was a boy called Richard Roissier, whose father was a colonel in the army and stationed in Germany. Richard, like me, was an only child and we both started at thirteen as new boys in Frank's house. While I was quite tall, about five foot seven, Richard was nearly six feet tall, so we were two large thirteen-year-olds and we became like brothers. Tragically, Richard was killed at the age of nineteen when on a summer's evening he fell off the back of a sports car in Earls Court. He was sitting on the back shelf and a taxi came round the corner, nicked the bumper, shook the car and he fell, hit his head on the road and was killed immediately. For me, this was the defining moment of growing up, and I cried for three days. He truly was the nearest thing I ever had to a brother.

I'll never forget the day Frank King called Richard and me, the two new boys, in for our sex talk. Frank was a pipe smoker, and his study had racks of pipes and stank of tobacco. He invited us in, he picked up his pipe and clenched it between his teeth.

'Now, boys,' he began. 'You've been in this house about three weeks now, and... er... this is the first time you will have been in a school where the majority of boys have got broken voices. I mean, they're nearly men.' Then, with the pipe still his mouth he continued. 'As you know it's only boys here and very occasionally in a school like this a senior boy may possibly come up and try and put his hand on your ...' at which point he struck a match and sucked on the pipe to light it, blew out the match, threw it away and started again. 'Now in a house like this, you get chaps who are almost going off to the army, I mean National Service is just round the corner. Occasionally some of the younger boys will be approached by one of these boys with the idea that they might go off and mmm – mmm- mmm- mmm ...' he sucked on his pipe again.

Richard and I were crying with silent laughter, but Frank never quite got to the point. Eventually the bell rang and with huge relief he blew out yet another match and said, 'OK chaps, is that all clear?' and off we went. So that was the sex talk from my housemaster!

Actually, it wasn't the first I'd had. The sex talk on the last day of term at my prep school was just as amusing. These are significant moments in a man's life. By then the clergyman had retired, so we had a chap who had been a housemaster at Fettes College and who came to St Neot's to see out his days as a prep school headmaster. He called twelve leavers into the drawing room. We all sat down, and he started telling us, 'Now boys, you're going off to your public schools and you need to know about the birds and the bees, and I'm going to illustrate it – with marrow plants, cross-pollination and bees.'

We all knew a thing or two and we had magazines under our mattresses – so we weren't having all this birds and bloody bees, cross-pollination nonsense. Being the bravest, I piped up, 'Enough about bees sir. What actually happens?'

'Well um … the man… the man puts his um thing inside a woman and … and… and a fluid comes out and he makes a baby,' he stuttered.

'No,' I thought. 'You're not getting away with that!' So I said, 'Fair enough. Tell me, sir. How do you know when the fluid's come out?'

He went slightly pink and muttered, 'Well, the man gets a mildly pleasant sensation.'

And I remember looking at him thinking, 'Yes, for you it probably is only a mildly pleasant sensation.' I'm happy to say that, even after all these years, it's been more than that where I'm concerned and continues to be so.

In later years, I found a letter to my father saying 'Dear Mr Collingwood, It's been such fun having Charles in the school and we do wish him best of luck at Sherborne. As you requested he has been informed of what happens in the next stage of life, so I'm sure that will carry him through.'

When it came to the birds and bees, my father was even worse. The nearest he came to giving me a sex talk was the beginning of the cricket term and he just said to me, 'Wear a box this term, old boy.' Stupidly, I didn't, and I got hit in the balls, which was bloody painful. I've worn a box ever since.

My lack of sex education didn't hamper my luck with the opposite sex. I was an early starter, getting engaged to a girl called Kirstine Meikle at Miss Greenup's. Her father was a master at Wellington College and we lived nearby. I used to go back and have tea at her house sometimes, and I loved her with the whole of my six-year-old heart. Unfortunately, I had to break the engagement off because she could run faster than me. I met Kirstine again when Judy and I were doing our show *Laughter and Intrigue* in Cheshire about five years ago.

At Sherborne, we were always writing letters to girls. On Valentine's Day, for example, it meant so much which one of us received the most cards, so we all wrote to every girl we knew who had our address, and hoped we'd get a pile of Valentines. Happily, I did a lot of the time.

It was, of course, absolutely forbidden to talk to girls. I think the rule at Sherborne then was that you were beaten if you were caught with a boy and expelled if you were caught with a girl. Seemed the wrong way round to me!

That's partly why I agree with my father, that it is healthier to be in a school in a town where you see girls and women other than your housemaster's wife and Matron. They say that boarding schools are absolutely rampant with homosexuality, and you can understand why if there are no girls about at all.

Actually, I rather fancied my Matron, who was gorgeous. I probably fancied all the maids that used to clean as well. God, they were lovely, but you know how it is with forbidden fruit.

Anyway, when I wasn't in The Remove, I was in 4E, which

was the class just before The Remove. I sat next to my best friend in the class, Jeremy Cox, who ended up as a very distinguished soldier in the Scots Guards, highly decorated for his work in Northern Ireland and very brave. I always say that the reason he was my best friend was that he was the only boy in the school who was more stupid than I was!

Presiding over this class was a terrifying man called Sam Hey, who had a face like a hippopotamus, bright red with a bald head, a big body and a very deep voice. As he got cross, he would rub his hands together more and more aggressively, before grabbing his cane to thrash one of us. Jeremy and I had quite a lot of fun hiding his cane and annoying him. We used to bury it or put it behind the bookcases and then bait him, and he'd get up to fever pitch wanting to beat us and, of course, he couldn't because he couldn't find the cane. Oh, simple minds!

The classroom window was just by Finger Lane, and the girls from Sherborne Girls' School, were always walking past. A few of us used to write love messages on paper aeroplanes and when Sam Hey's back was turned we'd fire them out of the window, so that they would land amongst the girls. How we longed for them to write back to us! But what you didn't want was the aeroplane not to make the window. If it was seen flying through the air by Sam Hey, that would mean a thrashing. Worse still, if it hit the wall and fell to the floor and he read the note – that didn't bear thinking about – so Jeremy and I made bloody sure they went through the window.

Sam Hey had never married, and lived with his mother in a rather elegant house in the town. Legend has it that a new boy came to Sherborne School who was very tiny, and was related to the Hey family. On his first Sunday, Mrs Hey, Sam's mother, with the best will in the world, invited this poor little wretch to tea. So this poor little boy is sitting there having tea with the most frightening schoolmaster in the south west of England, who is hugely disapproving of the fact that the boy's been asked to tea in the first place.

Sam's mother turned to the boy and said, 'Tell me, dear, did you cry on your first night at Sherborne?'

'No, Mrs Hey,' replied the boy politely. 'I didn't.'

'Good boy,' she said, then turned to Sam and said, 'You did, didn't you, dear?'

To which his deep voice replied, 'Shut up, mother!'

Contact with my parents was limited at Sherborne because there was no phone for us to use, but my mother would write so that I got a letter on a Monday and my father would write so I'd get a letter on a Friday. This worked very well because, while my father's letters were always very brief, we had fish for breakfast on a Friday and it was disgusting, so the fish was always slipped into the envelope that his letter had come in and put somewhere discreetly out of sight!

Looking back, they were happy if rebellious days, and it's a fine school. I'm now the proud president of the Old Boys' Association, so I must have done something right.

One very significant event occurred at home while I was away at Sherborne. On Whit Sunday 1958, our charming little cottage in Amport, near Andover burnt down. My father was there and a little boy had come round to play in the garden with our dog.

Suddenly the boy said, 'Your house is on fire!'

'I shall send you home with a smack if you're telling an untruth,' said my father. 'Because you must never make jokes like that.'

'No, Mr Collingwood! Come out and look!' The whole of the back of the thatched roof was one big burning mass.

My father rang the Andover fire brigade, who were on

holiday because it was Whit Sunday, so he rang Basingstoke and Winchester, both of which were just over fifteen miles away, but they said they'd come. The headquarters of RAF Maintenance Command was just up the road in Amport so, as a former RAF Officer, my father thought they might help. He rang them and asked for a fire truck.

'No, I'm terribly sorry, we can't because we may have a fire of our own,' was their reply.

'In that case,' said my furious father, 'just look out of your window and watch our house burn down!'

The house was one of eight little cottages that stood on the village green and they were absolutely beautiful, always being photographed for magazines. As it happens, the fire was taking hold when the local cricket team came back from practice. Many of them had been born in these cottages, but their families had moved when they built the council estate because they had upstairs lavatories there. They all knew my parents and appreciated how much they loved that house and, within seconds, they were on the roof relaying buckets and trying to dampen the flames. Unfortunately the water came from a well via an electric pump and my mother had to turn the electricity off, and the water ran out, so they piled into a bedroom and started chucking everything they could find onto the grass outside. My horrified parents were begging them to come out because the roof was about to fall in on them, but they risked their lives to help in any way they could.

By the time the fire brigade got there, the house next door had burnt down as well, and the village green was about four deep in cars with people who'd come to watch.

In the end, my father was looking at this smouldering wreck, which was now burnt down to the bottom windows, and a man in a deerstalker came up.

'Excuse me,' he said to my father, in a frightfully plummy voice. 'Are you the owner of this house?'

My father looked at him sadly and nodded. 'What's left of it, yes.'

'Keep a stiff upper lip old boy,' said the stranger. 'Keep a stiff upper lip.'

I remember my father saying to me, 'It's good advice, isn't it? I must keep a stiff upper lip. That will really help me over this.' Later he told me what really did help him over it, at least that first night. All his friends were so sorry for him they gave him whisky and he said, 'Your mother and I were completely plastered by about half past eight that night.'

That summer, we lived in a little borrowed caravan and a local farmer lent us his field and put an electric fence round it so that the cows couldn't get in. The only time my parents really got upset was the time they let our lovely Labrador, Damson, out of the caravan and she wouldn't come back. They called and called, and eventually my father got dressed and got into his car to drive round the lanes to see if he could find her. He drove past the house and there she was, sitting outside the back door waiting to be let in, and there was nothing there except the back door and a bit of wall.

Over time, they rebuilt the house and bought the one next door, which had also perished. When they finally finished it was beautiful.

THREE

First Love and RADA

By the time I left Sherborne I was in love. Georgia Taylor-Smith had been at Sherborne Girls' School and she was stunning. After we both left school, I was invited to stay with her family in their lovely house near Godalming. How I remember my first breakfast there. As I took the top off my egg they all stared at me.

'Do you like your egg?' someone asked.

'Yes, it's fine,' I said, puzzled by the keen interest.

'It's a pea-hen's egg,' they told me.

'Wow,' I thought. 'This is smart!' They had their own peacocks in the garden and that's where the egg had come from!

The romance with Georgia lasted through the summer of 1960 and into autumn, until she left to go to finishing school in Paris and I started teaching at a prep school in Buckinghamshire. A long relationship was never on the cards as far as her parents were concerned. Although they got on very well with my parents and with me, Georgia was always going to marry somebody a lot better off than I was.

Georgia's father had been partially blinded in an accident and only had peripheral vision. He had been an international sportsman, a mountaineer and a good golfer. He still went to London to work and he had a lovely wife and three gorgeous daughters, but at times you could sense his frustration. I was still a keen piano player and used to make pin money by playing in pubs at the weekends. Sometimes when I was staying with them, I would play the piano after dinner and, one evening, Georgia's father said, 'Charles, would it be possible for you to show me how to play?'

They had a wonderful grand piano in the drawing room, so I spent the evening carefully placing his hands on the piano keys, helping him to get the feel of them. We had such fun and goodness knows what time we went to bed that night. Happily, before Georgia and I went our separate ways, her father and I were able to sit at the piano together several times and repeat the exercise.

About twelve months after Georgia and I had last seen each other, I was on my way to a cricket match near Haslemere, in Surrey, in my mother's Mini. I was driving under a bridge when a sporty two-seater cut me up and pushed me into the side of the road. It was Georgia and she leapt out of the car and said, 'Charles, I thought it was you. What are you doing?'

'I'm playing cricket today at Cranleigh,' I answered.

'Come back afterwards,' she said. 'My parents would love to see you.'

So, cricket over, I went back and was greeted like the prodigal son. They'd put on a sumptuous meal, a couple of bottles of wonderful claret and they were keen to know what I was doing. After dinner, Georgia's father said, 'Charles, would you do me a favour? Would you play the piano to me?' I went in the drawing room to play the piano to him for a few minutes. When I finished there was a pause, and he said, 'May I play the piano to you now?' To my amazement he played beautifully – miles better than I would ever play. He was absolutely brilliant, I was choked. When he'd finished he said, 'Charles, you saved my sanity, because with your helping hands I've taught myself to play the piano.'

Sadly, I've not seen Georgia since that day. Her parents have probably passed away by now but I do hope that he managed to get twenty-odd happy years playing the piano to himself. Actually, when I was honoured on *This is Your Life* in 2003, my wife Judy worked very hard to try to get in touch with Georgia but to no avail. Shame, because I was very fond of Georgia and I still am, so it would have been lovely to see her.

As I mentioned before, my lack of academic success didn't prevent me taking a teaching post at a country prep school called Swanbourne House School in Buckinghamshire. I was seventeen and was employed in what would now be called a gap year, although it was actually two. Boys like me who were good at sport were taken on as dogsbodies, and to teach the tiniest ones in the school. So I taught geography, maths and English to the little ones, but I also ran the cricket, the football and the rugby, produced the plays and serviced the under-matron. All in a day's work.

It was a fantastic couple of years and I had a riotous time. I learnt to drive and I had three cars while I was there, my first being a 1936 Austin 7, which my father bought from his tailor for £25. That blew up going up a hill, so it was replaced with an Austin 10, which was in turn replaced by a 1937 Morris 12, in two-tone dark blue and black, with a running board. That car was a huge boost to the love life. As well as the under-matron, there were lots of other lovely ladies about, including one gorgeous married woman who was at least ten years older than me – God, she was sexy. She taught me so much, she put me off the younger woman for years.

I gave the vicar of Swanbourne a lift in my Morris once and he climbed into the passenger seat before I was able to warn him not to lean back. As soon as he sat down, the chair tipped right back onto the back seat, because it was used rather frequently in that position. It was quite tricky explaining to the vicar why he had ended up flat on his back with his legs up on the dashboard exclaiming, 'Oh, I say, your seat needs mending.'

'Actually,' I thought, 'it doesn't.'

From about November until about the end of March, the car wouldn't start because it was too old and the oil was too thick. Once it was started on the push in the morning, it would go for the day, so at school I tapped into an endless supply of helpers. Every day I would find six boys who had done something just naughty enough and tell them to report to Mr Collingwood's garage at eight o'clock the following morning for car-pushing duty.

Swanbourne had regular cricket matches against another smart prep school in Oxford called Summerfields, again a feeder for Eton. The masters used to come over and have lunch on match days, and there was one master called Porterhouse, with a very, very plummy voice. 'Come boy, come hee-ar,' he would say in his barking voice. The boys didn't seem to think much of him and they gave him the nickname, Fast Parson. I was intrigued to know why they were all saying, 'Look out, Fast Parson's coming, here comes Fast Parson.'

'Why do you call him Fast Parson?' I asked.

'Well you see, sir,' they replied. 'He teaches us Latin and he's always talking about the "fast parson singular"!'

During my time at the school, I taught the son of David Tomlinson, who you will know as the father in the films *Mary Poppins* and *Bedknobs and Broomsticks*. He was the most wonderful farceur and frequently starred in the West End with the likes of Robert Morley, Ian Carmichael and Nigel Patrick. He was one of the best light comedian actors that I'd seen and I admired him enormously. As an actor, if I could have waved a wand and been somebody else, I'd like to have been David Tomlinson. He knew absolutely everything about comedy timing, did the best double takes of anybody I've ever seen.

Of course, you will understand that by then I was thinking I was going to be an actor soon, and I was being advised that I should go to RADA (The Royal Academy of Dramatic Arts). Well, I'm not stupid – in fact somebody once said I was a calculating so-and-so – but if you're an aspiring actor who is teaching David Tomlinson's son, you are going to make pretty bloody sure that David Tomlinson thinks you're the nicest master in the school – and that his boy does too. David was very kind to me and during his son's last year at Swanbourne House, I often went to their house for supper with his wife, Audrey, and the other children. I discovered that David was quite a loose cannon as a person, but because his boy liked me, he liked me, and I was going to be an actor, so we had a common interest.

In my last term at Swanbourne, I was frequently going up to London for tuition, in preparation for my audition for RADA. I knew that this involved a three-minute modern piece and three minutes of Shakespeare, but I had no experience of acting at all. At Sherborne I had played cricket all the time, and I've never really been very interested in amateur acting. I've never wanted to rehearse for six weeks to do it for three nights and not be paid. I'd rather rehearse for three days and do it for six weeks and get paid.

Anyway, I was coached by a marvellous teacher at RADA called Denys Blakelock, who had written a book about auditions, which contained sample speeches. It was called *Choosing Your Piece* (only a sweet old queen called Denys Blakelock could write a book called that!). His crash course in acting was brilliant and he prepared me for my audition as Freddy from *The Deep Blue Sea* by Terence Rattigan, and Cassius from *Julius Caesar*. Fully armed, I went up to the audition.

Looking back on it now, I can't believe how naïve I was about the acting profession. I thought I'd just go along, do the audition and pass. Had I known that there were probably hundreds, if not thousands, that wanted one of the thirty-two places at RADA I'd probably have funked it, but as it was I did it and was told I'd have to wait three weeks for the result. In fact, after about five days David Tomlinson telephoned to say 'You're in.' He had rung John Fernald, who was the principal of RADA, to find out. I was so excited.

That winter, the end of 1962 and beginning of 1963, brought heavy snow and by then I was at the Academy and living in London. David was starring in *Boeing, Boeing* in the West End and, one Saturday evening when I was at a loose end, I went to see the show. Afterwards, I went backstage to his dressing room to compliment his performance and he said, 'What are you doing tonight, old thing? Come back with me and see Audrey and the children.' I didn't have to be back in London until Monday so I thought it was a splendid idea. We drove in his huge Rolls-Royce, with the number plate DT4, through Aylesbury towards his home, in Mursley, near Swanbourne House School, and as we reached the ridge above Winslow we were flagged down by the police. It had been snowing hard all the way from London and the roads were terrible.

'I'm sorry, Mr Tomlinson,' said the policeman. 'But you can't get any further. Down that hill there are four coaches and fourteen cars stuck in snow.'

'I've never not got home yet,' David protested.

'Well I'm afraid you're not going home by car, Mr Tomlinson, you're snowed under,' insisted the policeman.

'Right, old darling,' said David. 'We'll walk.'

So we reversed the car about a mile and parked on a garage forecourt, the police gave us a lift to where we'd been stopped and, in the clothes we were wearing and ordinary shoes, which were more suited to London than the snowbound countryside, we set off and walked the five-and-a-half miles to David's house. By now, it had stopped snowing; it was a clear night, there was a full moon and, in this vast white landscape, there was just us. I was nineteen years of age with the famous David Tomlinson by my side. He'd recently seen *Beyond the Fringe*, the memorable revue with Peter Cook, Dudley Moore, Alan Bennett and Jonathan Miller. He was particularly taken with one sketch, the 'Aftermyth of War', in which Peter Cook was an RAF Officer issuing an order to a pilot.

'Perkins?' he said.

'Yes, sir?'

'Get up in a crate, Perkins, pop over to Bremen and take a shufti.'

'Yes, sir.'

'Oh and Perkins ...'

'Yes, sir?'

'Don't come back.'

David thought that 'Don't come back' line was the funniest thing he'd ever heard. So mile after mile on this clear, frozen night, with nothing around us, he would say 'Perkins?'

'Yes, sir?' I replied.

'Get up in a crate, Perkins, pop over to Bremen and take a shufti.'

'Yes, sir.'

'Oh and Perkins ...'

'Yes, sir?'

'Don't come back.'

His laughter would echo round the countryside, there would then be a pause for another thirty seconds and I'd hear, 'Perkins?'

We got to his house at about half past five in the morning, after four-and-a-half hours in the snow. As, exhausted, we fell onto the gate, he turned to me and said, 'Charles, old darling, don't go and fuck the nanny now, will you?'

I wasn't to see David again until I'd been in *The Archers* a number of years. I was on my way to Birmingham to record *The Archers*, and was catching a train at Euston. As I walked down the platform a commuter train had just spewed its passengers onto the platform and hundreds of people were walking towards me, and there was this very tall, grey-haired, distinguished actor in amongst the crowd. He was head and shoulders above the rest and I recognized him immediately. As he came towards me I stood in front of him and said, 'David? Charles Collingwood.'

'Darling!' he said. 'I thought you were dead.' The crowd was pushing him along, and he called back over his shoulder, 'What are you doing?'

'I'm in *The Archers*,' I replied.

'Serves you right!' he shouted. Those were the last words we ever spoke to each other. But that was enough. That was two actors renewing their friendship. I don't think we needed to go and have lunch at the Garrick.

In the summer of 1962, as I prepared to start my new life at RADA, my parents rallied round to help. My father was used to the list of requirements for each educational establishment I'd attended, but this time, instead of three cricket shirts, four pairs of rugger socks, a pair of cricket boots and a bat, it said 'three singlets, two pairs of black tights, a pair of ballet pumps and fifteen sticks of make-up'! I can remember to this day my father standing in Anello & Davide, the theatrical costumier in Charing Cross Road, completely out of his depth, as the male shop assistant was gleefully fitting me up, rubbing his hands up and down my thighs and helping me into a pair of tights.

My place at RADA sorted, I then had to have somewhere to live. Being an only child I was now moving into a world that was totally alien to my parents, and they were anxious that I should have somewhere nice and safe to live. They travelled with me to look at a rented room in Hampstead, the first address we'd viewed, where we met my new landlady, Hilda Mary Lishman. I never called her Hilda or Miss Lishman; for the next forty years I simply called her Lishy. When we met she was still working, but was close to retirement.

Lishy raised the bar for me. Gradually over the time I spent as her lodger and young friend, I came to realize that for her, nothing in life was worth doing unless it was done to the highest standard. She taught me about the alternatives in life; vegetarian cooking, homeopathic medicine, the suggestion of reincarnation, and so much more. Above all she possessed a wisdom not encountered in any other person I have known. That wisdom was to help her alter the course of my life at a later date, but in those far off days she was a friend whose support and encouragement helped me through my time at RADA and, more importantly, through the many dark periods of the actor's curse: unemployment. Her belief in my ability helped me to remain an actor when I could so easily have opted out and taken a more secure path in life.

Lishy never owned a television; she despised it. She considered, rightly or wrongly, that almost everything on the small screen was third rate. But radio? That was quite different. Her love for Radio 4 knew no bounds, especially for radio drama and *The Archers*, so when I secured the part of Brian, her cup of joy overflowed. How she loved *The Archers*!

However, of all the art forms, theatre took centre stage and wherever I was performing, whatever the part, big, small or indifferent, Lishy would be there, in the front row of the stalls in a huge wide-brimmed hat, beaming from ear to ear. I was so pleased that during my time at RADA I was able to introduce her to my fellow student Ronald Pickup. In Ronald she saw a special something and she followed his every professional move just as closely as she did mine. We just avoided telling her when either of us was on television. Ronald and his family became very close to Lishy and, in her later years, generously entertained her at Christmas, a festival she refused to enjoy (it was a waste of time sending her Christmas cards, she never opened them). Like much of the modern world, Christmas had become too commercial for her.

Lishy never married and I know that over the years I became like the son she never had, and she became like a second mother to me. So it remained until the end of her life. Gradually, she grew into old age and I began to look after her, taking over her affairs. In her late eighties, life in Hampstead had become too hectic for her and, ever wise, she moved to the gentler life of Co. Kerry in Ireland. After several years living in a B&B overlooking Dingle Bay, Lishy made her last move to a nursing home nearby, where the most wonderful, patient nuns took care of her ever-increasing demands. Finally, at the age of ninety-eight, she died.

Judy and I were living in Muswell Hill when the phone rang at ten past three in the morning and this Irish voice said, 'Is that Charles?'

'Yes,' I said.

'Oh Charles, it's Sister Darrety here, I have to tell you, Mary died twenty minutes ago.'

'Oh, God,' I said.

'Yes,' she said. 'So I'll ring you in the morning.'

I put the phone down and thought, 'But you just rang!' Sad as it was, I had to laugh. It was so wonderfully Irish.

In Ireland at that time, you could only be cremated in Dublin, so the nuns promised to dress Lishy in her prettiest frock and her coffin was driven to the Fair City where, in the chapel, I read her favourite poem, 'The Fiddler of Dooney', by W. B. Yeats. Dear Lishy wouldn't have a priest anywhere near her and didn't want anybody other than Judy and me at the funeral. We were the only mourners, except for a stranger in the crematorium who crossed himself the whole time because there wasn't a priest and he thought she would go to hell!

'Who's that bloke in the sports jacket and those cavalry twill trousers?' asked a RADA student who was in the year above me, a few weeks after I started. When told it was one Charles Collingwood he quipped, 'He's the first country squire we've ever had here!'

Thrilled and surprised to be accepted into this wonderful institution, I turned up with my very posh accent to enter a whole new world. I remember being told about the voice coach and thinking, 'What do you mean voice lessons? Why do I need voice lessons?'

Halfway through my first term I almost came unstuck. Students had two tests, consisting of part of a Shakespeare play in the early part of the term and something more modern in the latter, and they were both judged. Well, I'd never done any Shakespeare in my life and I was so self-conscious in my black tights and my ballet pumps that all I did was giggle. I thought I was doing all right, but when it came to the adjudication at half-term, Paul Lee, a jobbing actor who was teaching at the Academy, went round all the others and gave them all their critiques, leaving me out. 'Oy, oy! What about me?' I asked.

'God, I was so hoping you wouldn't ask!' he said, putting his head in his hands. Then he proceeded to destroy me with, 'That was the worst thing I've ever seen. What are you doing here? What was that supposed to be?'

Ever the arrogant youth, I was looking over my shoulder thinking he must mean somebody sitting behind me. Sadly not.

By then I was quite popular because I made everybody laugh, so when we all went to the pub, my fellow students bought me drinks and commiserated. But I was absolutely certain it was the end of the line, because if you didn't get it right at RADA you were out. Of the thirty-six that started I think only eighteen of us lasted the whole two years, and you really had to watch your step. For example, unlike most universities, they'd kick you out if you were late more than three times in the term – and quite right too because ours is a very exacting profession. You can't be late for a performance.

Even for pre-recorded radio, like *The Archers*, you have to be punctual. I'll never forget the experience of one poor actor. Many years ago, Harry Littlewood played Ronnie Beddows, a barman in The Bull. On the day of one recording, he got on the train and when the ticket collector came round to clip his ticket, he said, 'Sorry sir, this train is non-stop to Manchester. It doesn't stop at Birmingham.'

'But I've got to be there by lunchtime!' spluttered Harry. 'I'm recording *The Archers*.'

'Sorry, sir,' repeated the guard. 'You'll have to go to Manchester and get a train back to Birmingham.'

Poor Harry was panic-stricken but he thought on his feet. He went into the lavatory, somehow managed to unscrew the metal hook from the back of the door and wrote a note saying, 'Please phone the BBC and tell them I'm on wrong train.' Then he wrapped the note round the hook, securing it with a rubber band. As the train passed through Birmingham New Street, hurtling along at breakneck speed, Harry opened the window and lobbed this lethal weapon out. The hook scudded across the platform like a tracer and, frankly, he was lucky it didn't kill someone.

After an arduous journey, the frazzled actor made it to Pebble Mill at around teatime, thinking life was over and he had blown his chance. As he walked into the studio, he found everybody was still laughing. Someone had indeed found his note and followed his instructions and the cast and crew thought it was the funniest thing they'd heard for years.

Back to RADA and, after Paul's demolition job I thought 'Shit, I'm struggling here.' Then came the second half of the term and we were to perform an excerpt from Chekhov's *Three Sisters*. I was cast as the old family retainer Chebutykin, who goes through something of a crisis during the play but is quite a funny old boy, so I thought, 'All I can do is try to make people laugh, so I'm going to make him comic.' I really worked at this. The director was a sour old bag who didn't like me because I was trying to make it comic and, as far as I could see, she thought everything in life should be tragic. As the performance loomed, I felt more and more isolated, convincing myself that I was only going to be there a term and thinking, 'I shall have to tell David Tomlinson I didn't hack it and tell my parents to pay back the grant.'

Finally, the fateful night arrived and the show was judged by John Fernald, the principal. Afterwards, we were called into his office where he looked sternly over his glasses and said this was one of the worst first-term intakes he'd ever had at the Academy. He was not pleased with what he'd seen etc., etc. Then he said, 'But there's one beaming, glittering exception, and that was you, Charles.'

'Me?'

'I thought it was individual, well thought out and very funny,' he continued. 'You really made something of the character.'

Of course, I floated out on cloud nine, while the old bag sat in the corner scowling furiously. That was a defining moment in my whole life as an actor. Someone had belief in me – and not just anybody. Fernald was of the theatre, and considered to be a great Chekhovian director at that time. If he thought my performance in Chekhov was good, I must be on to something.

In fact, throughout the next two years at the Academy, the bell would ring in the classroom or rehearsal room, and whoever was teaching us would answer the phone and say, 'Charles, Mr Fernald wants to see you.' I always thought I was about to be handed the black spot. I would go down to his study, heart thumping, knock on the door and hear his plummy voice saying, 'Come in.' I would put my head round the door and say, 'You wanted to see me, Mr Fernald?' and he would crack up. 'Ha, ha, ha ha, ha – just wanted to see the face!'

Obviously, he just thought I had something funny about me, which was delightful, so I played funny parts in every show we put on. In one production, I walked onto the stage and I hadn't opened my mouth before I could hear him laughing.

Having come from the country I knew nothing whatsoever about the ways of showbiz but I had noticed there were quite a lot of camp people about. Actually, they looked frightfully glamorous to me and I thought, 'That is obviously the way you crack it – ponce about a bit.' One day, I was walking down the passage and Mr Fernald's voice boomed out after me, 'Stop mincing, Collingwood!' I have to say, by and large, this is a note I have taken through life, and mincing is not part of my make-up.

My contemporaries, who included Hywel Bennett and Bruce Myers, had all spent time in thespian groups such as the

National Youth Theatre and the National Student Drama Festival, and were almost semi-pro. I'd just come up from the country thinking I'd be an actor, so I was little wet behind the ears. Nevertheless, the three of us were great friends and we would howl with laughter together.

Bruce is a wonderful actor from Manchester who has enjoyed a very successful career and worked for many years with Peter Brook in Paris and all over the world. Hywel was always going on about how Welsh he was, although as far as we were concerned he was an oik from Streatham. Even then, we could see he was going to be successful, because he was very ambitious and, of course, he went on to find fame and fortune as TV's *Shelley*. I've never been very ambitious myself; calculating, yes, ambitious, no.

Gabrielle Drake, who has also had a glamorous and distinguished career, was a great friend of mine. She had also been to a private school, so I was the posh bloke and she was the posh girl.

I was invited to Gabrielle's twenty-first birthday party at the Savoy Hotel, and I sat opposite a friend of hers, a girl in the palest pink dress. As I gazed across the table I thought, 'You are actually the most beautiful woman I have ever seen and you're going to marry me and nobody else. You're mine!'

At the Savoy in those days they used to announce, 'Ladies and Gentlemen, it's cabaret time' and, from the dance floor, the stage would rise up three feet. I was sitting there looking at my future wife, when Tommy Cooper appeared, walked to the front of the stage and said, 'Good evening.' Then he said 'I can always tell, in three seconds, if I like an audience or not. Goodnight.' And he walked off – we didn't see him for another half an hour.

I cried with laughter because I loved Tommy Cooper and that had been the bravest opening to an act I'd ever seen.

Eventually he came back and I fell about throughout his entire performance. When it was over, the stage went down, the lights came up, and this beautiful girl sitting opposite me, who I was going to marry, just said, 'Well, he's the most boring man I have ever listened to.' Suddenly, I couldn't see what was attractive about her at all.

Appalled, I thought I must get out of there, so I went and had a pee and stood next to Tommy Cooper. Suddenly there's this giant of a man, my hero, next to me but I didn't talk to him. I was just so thrilled that I had peed next to Tommy Cooper.

My own twenty-first proved to be a disappointment. Another fellow RADA student was Ian Ogilvy, who had a pale blue Sunbeam Alpine, which I fiercely coveted. For several months before my twenty-first birthday my father had been asking the same question.

'Do you like the new MG sports car?'

'Yes I do, father,' I'd say, thinking, 'Come on twenty-first!'

'I like the pale blue,' he said.

'So do I,' I eagerly agreed, adding, 'I like all the colours actually, father. I don't mind what colour it is.'

'No, I love pale blue.'

'Good for you, father.'

On my birthday, Saturday, 30 May, 1964, I got the train down to Andover and when I arrived at the house my parents handed me a glass of champagne. It was a glorious day, we were sitting outside and my mother handed me this wonderful little box.

'Yes!' I thought. 'Car key inside!' I was so excited, and I opened this box and there was a watch. My face fell. To this day, I cringe because I know they saw the disappointment in my face. I took out this wonderful watch, which they'd had engraved, and I thought, 'Still not going to get the birds off Ian Ogilvy, is it?' I would like to point out that by now the car would have been scrap for many, many years but the watch still runs beautifully and I wear it with pride. It's an Omega Sea Master de Ville, so it is probably worth fifty times what they paid for it. A lesson for life!

My father had a bit of tummy trouble that day. In fact, he was always having tummy trouble. Even so, he bravely said, 'Come on, we're going out to dinner, there's a lovely place near Newbury.' We all got togged up, drove over to the restaurant and my father drank a little more than he should have done. Halfway through dinner he fled from the table, rushed to the loo and was as sick as a dog, so my twenty-first birthday ended before pudding, with me driving home, wearing a watch I didn't like very much, and my father in the back groaning, as my mother cradled his head on her shoulder. Not exactly a party to remember.

Knowing my love of stand-up comics, one Saturday night Hywel Bennett challenged me to enter a talent contest in a pub in Tooting Bec. 'You're bound to win it,' he assured me. So, innocently, I went along and said to the landlord, 'Can I enter your talent contest?'

It was the roughest of pubs. In fact, I wouldn't dare walk past it now in daylight, let alone go into it on a Saturday night. It was full of sailors and some other tough-looking characters. When it was my turn, I tapped the microphone and asked for silence.

'Quiet, please, quiet. Ssh,' I said. 'I haven't come here not to be heard.' Well, by God, you could have heard a pin drop then; you've never heard anything so quiet in your life. 'I'm going to tell a joke,' I said.

'One filthy word,' shouted the landlord, 'and I shall throw you bodily out of the pub.'

'It's not filthy at all,' I told him. 'A teacher comes into a classroom and says, "Right children, I want you to open your books" and a little boy interrupts, "Teacher, teacher! Is God in this room?"

"Yes, darling. God is in this room. Now open your book at page …"

"Teacher, teacher! Is God around my desk?"

"Yes, sweetheart. God is around your desk. Now, on page 15 you'll see that …"

"Teacher, teacher! Is God *on* my desk?"

"Yes, he's on your desk. Now page …"

"Teacher, teacher! Is God in my inkwell?"

"Yes, he's in your inkwell."

And the boy stuck his hand over the inkwell and said, "Got him!"'.

I thought that was quite funny. On a Saturday night in Tooting Bec? Nothing! Not even a titter. *Total* silence. So, in a moment of blind panic, and relieved to see a piano in the corner, I said, 'I shall now finish my act by doing an impression of Fats Waller!' (I can't do an impression of Fats Waller.)

I left the stage to the sound of my own footsteps. But while I was linking between the story and Fats Waller, I imagined the sailors sharpening their knives, and spotted Hywel Bennett crawling underneath the tables, making for the exit at the back before we were hung, drawn and quartered. Unfortunately, I had to go and sit with the other contestants in the front row and wait for the judging. I came last, and was given a booby prize of a miniature bottle of whisky, which I drank on the tube from Tooting Bec to Hampstead. A steep learning curve.

Years later, I went to audition for a season at the Marlowe Theatre, Canterbury, and I told that story as my audition speech. I embroidered it rather and made it more theatrical but it got me the job because the director thought it was a hilarious, self-denigrating improvisation. Little did he know it was true!

His name was David Kelsey and he appeared only to want the company of gay people. He rang my agent and booked me, then he rang every actor he knew who knew me.

'Of course, Charles is gay, isn't he?' he asked.

'No,' they said.

'Well, he was camp as anything when he came for the audition.'

'He might be,' they told him. 'But he'll work his way through Canterbury – and it won't be the blokes.'

When I showed up for work, he wouldn't talk to me for the first three weeks, because I was like some alien being.

In my final year at RADA, we put on a show at the Vanburgh called *Ever Since Aeschylus*, which was a kaleidoscope of theatre through the ages, to celebrate the Academy's first sixty years. This we performed before Her Majesty the Queen and the HRH Queen Mother.

There was a man in my class who, to make money while he studied, drove a minicab, and he was fiercely anti-royal. He was appalled when he was told he had to be in the show, and at the dress rehearsal we were instructed that, as the Queen was about to leave the stage, we would giving three cheers for Her Majesty. He reacted very aggressively. Nothing would make him cheer the Queen, he wasn't going to do it and that was that. We all sighed a bit but that evening, in front of a distinguished audience, we did the show and, after the curtain call, the Queen came on stage. It was the first time any of us had been that close to the Queen and, having shaken all our hands, she reached the end of the line and guess what? Our anti-royalist was the one who started the three cheers. It just proved what an effect royalty can have on people.

Another memory of my RADA days was our summer production of *Measure for Measure* in the open air theatre at

Holland Park. This allowed me to combine my love of cricket with my love of theatre, and I soon had the company turning up early to play tennis-ball cricket in the park. Terry Hands, Ronnie Pickup and all the others, even the girls, began to enjoy it so much that it became almost more important than the show and we continued to play backstage long after the play had begun. Actors could hear their cues coming up but would continue to bat, almost missing their entrance, and I'm quite sure that every now and then the ball sailed over the set onto the stage. Years later I read an interview with Terry Hands, by then a hugely successful theatre director, who said, 'Now to relax actors before rehearsals in the morning I like them to play cricket in the aisles of the theatre.' I thought, 'You stole that from me, you sod!'

Towards the end of my time at RADA I became apprehensive about the future. Would I be able to hack it as an actor out in the real world? I was becoming increasingly nervous at the prospect. Little did I know it then but I would soon have something else to be nervous about. I was about to meet my first wife, Jenny.

FOUR

A Brief Marriage

Before I returned to RADA for my last term, my parents took me with them on holiday to the South of France. On the first morning at the Cavalière Sur Plage Hotel, I was sitting on the beach and saw this pretty girl in the sea, and I thought 'Wow'. I was rather on my own, so I went and had a little swim and said 'Hello.'

She said, 'Hello,' and there we were, treading water in about forty fathoms and having a chat. I asked her who she worked for and she said, 'The Queen.'

'Hang on!' I thought. 'I'm in here.' Not unlike my grandfather, who didn't do a hands turn, I thought, 'If she works for the Queen I'm on to a good thing. And if I can get in with Princess Anne, I'm absolutely made.' So I said, 'Do you want to come out for a drink?'

I took her out that evening and then I discovered she worked for the *Queen* magazine, and not actually Her Majesty the Queen, which slightly took the gilt off it. But she was good fun, I was very naïve and she was too. One thing led to another.

Jenny's family lived in Surrey and, socially, she was exactly the sort of person I thought my parents would approve of. When it came to her parents – well let's put it this way, I liked her father.

As luck would have it, Terry Hands had just set up the Everyman Theatre in Liverpool with Peter James, another distinguished theatre director, and Martin Jenkins, who later became a top radio director. When I graduated, in the winter of 1963, they were casting a production of *Waiting for Godot* and I got the part of Estragon, one of the two tramps. It was my first professional part and it was about as good a part as you can get. It was absolutely fantastic. I was also to play Ross in the company's production of *Macbeth*.

The wage was £10 a week, and out of that we had to find our digs, so there wasn't a lot of change. Terry's philosophy for Liverpool, which I thought was a sound one, was that a young actor will take £10 a week. If you find an actor of fifty who's prepared work for £10 a week, they can't be very good. Among the cast were Susan Fleetwood, John McEnery, David Bailie, Bruce Myers, Terence Taplin and Philip Manikum, most of them fresh out of drama school.

Up I went to Liverpool, where I found digs in Toxteth, not far from the Anglican Cathedral. I had a little kitchenette, and another room with a bed and wonderful old-fashioned furnishings. Next to the gas fire was a meter into which I fed shillings and two shillings and on the next floor down was the bathroom, which also had a meter for the hot water. It was a very cold winter and every time I had a bath I had to pad my way down a freezing cold passage into the bathroom and fill the dreaded meter with shillings to get about three inches of hot water. Then back along the freezing corridor to feed my gas fire with more shillings.

The landlady said, as they all did then, 'No visitors allowed', meaning you couldn't have girls back. I was thinking, 'God, I'm going to have a bit of a struggle here,' but, in fact, it was only Jenny who would be coming because I was actually rather faithful to her. She used to come up from London to visit, and I had to smuggle her into the digs. On occasions the landlady would stand outside my room calling, 'I'm sure you've got somebody in there.'

'No, no, no, Mrs Willow,' I lied. 'I'm here all on my own.'

Terry Hands was playing Macbeth. Now Terry, by his own admission, is not the best actor, and he might say neither am I, but we've both done all right. One day, during a coffee break in rehearsals I remember doing a cod performance of his Macbeth, while the cast fell about laughing. Terry had left to go to his office and, unfortunately for me, returned in time to see the tail end of my impression. He was not hugely impressed, so it possibly wasn't a major career move for me. I've certainly not worked for him since, although I've admired him enormously from afar.

Living in Liverpool had the effect of leaving me pining for Jenny, absence obviously making the heart grown fonder. I would smuggle her up as often as I could, to the disapproval of her parents, I'm sure. I could only hack it for a while; it was a pretty Spartan existence and I lost a lot of weight, so I left and returned to the south to begin a number of years when, apart from the odd spit and a cough on the telly, I considered myself to be out of work.

My first taste of the West End stage came along straight after I left the Everyman, in 1965. I was cast to understudy Alan Bates in an Arnold Wesker play called *The Four Seasons*. It was a two-hander, co-starring Diane Cilento, who at that time was married to Sean Connery, and her understudy was Jean Trend, who was later to star for many years in another radio soap, *Waggoner's Walk*. I was much younger than Alan and, had anything happened to him, my first speech in the West End would have been nine pages long!

I had hardly learned the nine pages before the notice went up that the play was coming off. It was a massive flop. I don't know why, because it was beautifully written. My memory of it is now vague, except that I do vividly remember, in one act, there was a great theatrical *tour de force* where Alan Bates made a real apple strudel. He mixed the dough, rolled it out, filled it with raisins and apple, rolled it up and cooked it, and then ate some of it on stage; it was pretty spectacular. As a malnourished understudy I used to eat what was left in the wings. Alan might go off to the Garrick for dinner, but I was an impoverished actor and free apple strudel every night did me nicely.

Sadly, as I said, after about two weeks we were all called into the circle bar. The production staff, Alan, Diane, Jean, myself and the playwright, Arnold Wesker, gathered round and the news of the closure was confirmed to us. The atmosphere was very solemn and nobody said a word. However, I was a team player: I've always tried to be optimistic and look on the bright side. So there I was, in my twenties, my first time in the West End, no experience, with Alan Bates, major star, Diane Cilento, major star married to James Bond, and nobody wants to hear the opinion of one of the understudies.

'Can I say something?' I piped. You could have heard a pin drop. 'I think it's really, really awful that it's coming off,' I blundered on, 'because that apple strudel scene is absolutely fantastic.' Naïve gumph continued to spill out of my mouth.

When I'd finished, Arnold Wesker, who's about four foot eight when he's in heels, jumped out of his seat, his face puce, and screamed, 'You little wanker. It is that *fucking* apple strudel scene that's killed the *fucking* play, you little tit!'

I slumped back in my seat and an edit button came on in my head saying, 'Be a bit more cautious next time, Charles. Boy did you fail on that one.' I buried my head. I didn't dare look at anybody. I can't actually remember anything that happened afterwards. I wish I could say Alan came up and said 'There we are, dear boy, come and have lunch at The Ivy', but I think they all sent me to Coventry, quite rightly, for being a naïve little twerp. That was my first brush with mixing with anyone famous, and not long after that I was sacked by my agent.

While at RADA, I'd been courted by agents called Fraser and Dunlop. Peter Dunlop was very correct and gave the appearance of a City gent, while Jimmy Fraser was a truly camp Scotsman. With a dainty wave he said, 'There's a million pounds in that smile.' There may have been when I was relaxed, but when he took me to fancy parties to meet big producers and urged me to show off my smile, some terrible sort of rictus grimace came onto my face. By the time *The Four Seasons* ended, our relationship was cooling a bit because he'd tried to get to know me better in a lift once, and I wasn't playing that game.

It was left to Peter Dunlop, the other half of Fraser and Dunlop, to break the bad news. He summoned me to his office and, sitting in the corner, was one of his assistants, a waspish little man who was filing his fingernails while Peter Dunlop proceeded to sack me from the agency.

'Charles, old boy, you're not part of the theatre world really,' he said, rather patronizingly. 'I know you've been to RADA and you're a fine young actor, but you went to a good school. Why don't you get a job in the City? I'm afraid your career is not with us.'

I glanced at his assistant in the corner, still filing his nails and smiling at me as if to say, 'You're not one of us, dear'. Peter wished me well, handed me my photographs and, a minute later, I was in Regent Street with no agent, no work, nothing.

Now spool the whole film forward about thirty years: I'd been in *The Archers* a long time, had a good career in television, and Judy and I were living in our comfortable house in Muswell Hill. One hot June day we decided to have a lunchtime barbecue by the pool, so I offered to go to the shop round the corner to buy some salad and a cold bottle of white wine. As I walked up the street, Peter Dunlop's assistant who, all those years ago, had been sitting by his side looking down his nose at me shuffled round the corner, nothing more than a drunken vagrant. I've often been asked if I said hello, but I'm afraid the Good Samaritan doesn't stretch that far with me. But there are certain faces you never forget, and that was one of them.

Jenny and I somehow drifted into an engagement. We felt we were in love and I suppose, in a very naïve way, we were. She was only seventeen when I met her, I was twenty-one, and I wasn't earning much. Her parents tolerated the fact that I wanted to be an actor, but I'm not sure they were at all thrilled at the imminent nuptials.

The wedding, on 22 September 1967, was at Worplesdon church in Surrey. It was arguably the second biggest wedding since the Queen and Prince Philip. We had plain-clothes policemen guarding the presents and I seem to remember there were nineteen casserole dishes, which was mildly excessive. I have to say, when we got divorced I'm jolly glad I didn't get nine and a half of them.

We set up home in a little top-floor flat just off the Edgware Road in Kendall Street, with a fearsome landlady whom we loathed. She was a dreadful old bat whose name I can't remember, thank God.

In Kendall Street, there was a lovely fruit and veg shop called Tropical Fruits, run by a man called Monty Newman and his wife. We were regular customers there, buying avocado pears, melons and peaches, but one day Monty said to me, 'Charles, is everything all right with you?'

'Yes,' I said. 'Why?'

'You don't seem to be buying so many avocados now,' he observed shrewdly. 'You tend to come in here and ask for one potato. Are things tough?'

'Bloody right they are,' I said. 'I haven't worked for six months.'

'Do you fancy working here?' he asked.

'Not half, Monty!' I said.

'Be here at 7.30 tomorrow morning,' he said.

So the following day I proudly put on my Tropical Fruits jacket and worked for Monty Newman. I always hoped if I was ever the subject of *This is Your Life*, which I never dreamt I would be, that Monty would be alive, because I would have wanted him as a guest. He and his wife were incredibly kind to me as an out-of-work actor.

My agent would ring the shop and say, 'Charles needs to go for an audition.'

'Drop that, Charles,' Monty would say. 'And good luck.'

In fact, when I did get a break in children's television and stopped working for them, they couldn't have been sweeter.

I have two abiding memories from that job. One is the first time I rode the Tropical Fruits' delivery bicycle around Marble Arch with a big box of fruit and vegetables in the crate at the front, I leant the handlebars over to the right slightly going round Marble Arch. It was at that point I realized that the fruit and veg were so heavy I couldn't straighten the handlebars. As far as I can remember I cycled round Marble Arch for three and a half days.

The second memory from Tropical Fruits was when I was delivering fruit and veg to a nearby block of flats. I pushed the entry doorbell and this rather fierce woman said, 'Yes?'

'Er, Tropical Fruits here, madam,' I called.

'OK, press the bell for the seventh floor.' At the seventh floor, there she was, standing by the door.

'Take it down into the kitchen, last door on the left, and put it on the table.'

I went into the kitchen, carrying the box in both hands and there on the table where I wanted to put the box was her handbag. So I put a corner of the box on the table, picked up her handbag in my left hand, pushed the box on with my right – and at that moment she walked in the door. All she saw was me with her handbag in my hand, and I knew I'd had it. There was no way I could say 'I wasn't stealing anything out of your handbag, I was ...' and if I didn't say anything she would think I was stealing something out of her handbag anyway. I used to get a lot of tips, but I sure as hell didn't get one that day.

Another job I had was cleaning other people's houses. There was a very enterprising actor who created a cleaning agency, called Domestics Unlimited, which employed out-of-work actors. One summer's day – the day of the Ladies' Singles Finals at Wimbledon, actually – I was, maddeningly, booked at the last minute to go and clean the Countess of Strafford's silver in Cheyne Walk, where my grandfather had once had a house. Jenny had a car so I borrowed it and drove to Cheyne Walk, furious that I couldn't watch the tennis. I parked outside the front door, rang the bell and a fuming housekeeper appeared and demanded, 'Who are you?'

'I've come to clean the Countess's silver,' I said.

'You don't ring the front doorbell! You come to the tradesmen's entrance,' she replied, snootily.

'I'm very sorry,' I said. 'I didn't know about that.'

'And you *don't* park your car outside the front door, either. You park it over there,' she continued. 'Who the hell do you think you are?'

Eventually, this very cross housekeeper said, 'Come into the kitchen at once,' so in I went. Now, I had thought she'd have a few little bits and pieces of silver, like me, and I'd have it done in ten minutes. Well, there was about four miles, five feet deep of silver. My first thought was, 'Oh God, this is going to take until six o'clock, I've had it for the tennis.' So I picked up a cloth, with the housekeeper hovering behind me. 'Do you mind awfully if I pop to the car and bring in a little radio so I could listen to the tennis?' I asked.

'Sit down and do as you're told,' she snapped. 'Just get on with cleaning the silver.'

'Well, would it be all right if I had a cigarette?' I asked a few minutes later.

'A cigarette! In the Countess's kitchen? How dare you!' she exploded.

So, there I was cleaning the silver, getting more and more irate and wanting to kick the lights out of this bloody woman, when from the garden on this beautiful summer's day appeared this most wonderfully attractive, early middle-aged lady, in a sarong and a bathing suit. She came up to me and said, 'What's your name? Are you an actor as well?'

'Yes,' said I. 'I'm Charles Collingwood.'

'Oh my dear. Good Lord, what a lot you've got to do. Let me help you,' she said. 'I'm the Countess of Strafford.'

'Oh, how lovely.' I managed. She pulled up a chair and I thought to myself, 'I'm going to play my two ace cards now,' so I said, 'Excuse me, Countess, would you mind awfully if I had a cigarette?'

'My darling!' she said. 'Could I steal one of yours? I've left mine in the garden.' She took one of my cigarettes and, over her shoulder, she called out to the housekeeper, 'Have you got a match?'

'Thank you,' I said politely as this furious woman came over to light our cigarettes. We started puffing on the cigarettes and I thought 'I've got one more card to play', so I said, 'Do forgive me, it's terribly impertinent I know, but it's the final of the

Ladies' tennis and I've got a little radio in the car. Would you mind awfully if I brought ...'

'My darling, of course it is,' she said. 'Leave all that. Come into the drawing room at once. Let's go and watch it.' And, over her shoulder, she called to the housekeeper 'And bring us some tea and some cakes, won't you?'

So I watched the tennis with the Countess of Strafford, and then I went back and cleaned the silver, but I never saw the housekeeper again!

Market research was another, rather demoralizing, way of earning a few bob. On one raw February day when the weather changed from snow, to sleet, to rain and back again, I was doing market research outside a pub in Acton. I was wearing a very old threadbare donkey jacket and carrying a clipboard and a pencil, stopping appropriate people to ask them their age and their social group and whether they had a drink before breakfast or whatever it was. It was three o'clock in the afternoon and I was frozen to the marrow, when I heard the pub door shut behind me. Then I felt a tug at my sleeve. I looked down and there was this dear little old lady.

'Excuse me, dear,' she said 'Have you got sixpence for a cup of tea?'

'No, no I haven't,' I said, trying to shake her off. 'Please leave me alone, please, just let me get on with my job. Just go away.'

After a moment's pause, I felt another tug on my arm, and she said, 'No dear, I meant have *you* got sixpence for a cup of tea?'

And I thought, 'How sad do I look?'

From our flat off the Edgware Road, Jenny and I moved to a little cottage in Ealing called Kerrison Villas, which my mother-in-law used to call Kerosene Villas. Fair enough; in a strong westerly we could smell the aircraft fuel from Heathrow. To be honest, my father wasn't much better. He refused to write Ealing when he was sending us a letter, because he said 'Nobody lives in Ealing'. He always insisted it was London W5. Later, when I moved to Muswell Hill, he always used to write 'Highgate'.

For the most part, I got on all right with my in-laws after the wedding, but we had some strange times. One really good memory I have of the family is the day they invited me to Trooping the Colour. Jenny's father had got tickets and, all dressed up, we got a taxi to Horse Guards Parade. On the way, we saw a very hot and bothered American running along the pavement. Jenny's father stuck his head out and said, 'Are you going to Trooping the Colour?'

'Sure am,' replied the American.

'Hop in, I'll give you a lift,' said Jenny's father.

'Hey thanks,' said the American. 'I'm so grateful to you. This Trooping the Colour, it starts about eleven o'clock, doesn't it?'

'No,' retorted my father-in-law. 'It doesn't start *about* eleven o'clock, it starts *at* eleven o'clock.'

How very British.

Trooping the Colour is a wonderful spectacle, but I tend to notice the small details. I remember seeing one Grenadier Guard at the furthest point from the Queen, marching along and then suddenly scratching an itch on the end of his nose.

Afterwards, as we walked down the Mall, on our way to Madame Prunier's, the renowned fish restaurant in St James's Street, Concorde flew for the first time at about three hundred feet over Buckingham Palace. It was a good day.

Another occasion sticks in my mind for quite different reasons. My in-laws were kind enough to invite my parents for Christmas, along with my dear maiden aunt Jane. They arrived in my mother's Mini. When they got out of the car, my mother gave me a kiss and said, 'Darling I've bought Joan this.' (Joan being my mother-in-law). She showed me an azalea, which was a very nice azalea, about a foot high in a pot.

'I think that's lovely, mother.' I said. I couldn't bring myself to say, 'When you go up the stairs, on the first landing is an azalea tree, which is about fifteen feet high, and I've never seen anything that will be confined to a downstairs lavatory as quickly as your azalea.' How right I was: by teatime that was in the loo.

One weekend, when I had been out of work for a while, Jenny and I went to a dance at the home of a friend of her parents. There were a lot of Hooray Henrys present. I was sitting alone with a whisky, rather depressed, unemployed and feeling sorry for myself, when my mother-in-law came to me.

'Charles,' she said. 'What are you doing?'

'I'm just having a moment to myself, Joan.'

'What's the matter with you?' she asked. 'Good God, you're supposed to be an entertainer, why aren't you entertaining everybody?'

Jenny was dancing with some chinless wonder so I thought, 'Right'. I went to the downstairs loo and I took all my clothes off, except for my pants, which I tucked like a G-string up my arse, and I walked out of the loo, got hold of Jenny and said 'Dance with me!' She screamed.

The next thing I knew I'd got a horrified mother-in-law standing beside me hissing, 'Charles! What do you think you are you doing?'

'I'm entertaining everybody!' I said.

The marriage to Jenny lasted five years. It all went pear-shaped at Christmas 1971, and around that time I met Judy Bennett, the love of my life.

Judy and I met while we were in Bristol doing a children's

television series called *Words and Pictures*. I remember walking down the corridor of the train and Judy, in a purple mini-dress and high-heeled boots, was walking in front. The train induced a sort of wiggle in her and I remember thinking, 'Ooh, how lovely'. But she was married with two boys, so I was never going to go anywhere near her.

It was only when my marriage started to disintegrate and I discovered that her marriage was falling apart too, that we started taking each other a bit more seriously. In the autumn of 1971, we were recording the show and I said to Judy, 'I'm just going to ring Jenny because she's just been to a job interview today.'

I have a tendency to be rather forward-looking in my life, which drives Judy mad, because I'm always thinking what I'm going to do tomorrow or next month rather than today. I'm a planner, and I knew my marriage was going to come to an end, and that I couldn't get through another Christmas with the azaleas and the mother-in-law, or another twelve months with a woman I was no longer in love with. So I had said to Jenny, 'Why don't you get a job' because, in a rather calculating way, I thought, 'When I tell you the marriage is over I think you should have a job. That way you're not stuck at home, you've got to go somewhere.'

Anyway, I went down to Bristol and she had to go for this interview in Acton so I rang her and asked how she'd got on.

'Actually, I think I've got the job,' she said.

'Oh good,' I said. 'What's the company?'

'They're in drink vending, and they dispense coffees and teas out of one of those machines,' she said.

'And what's the company called?' I asked.

'Breakmate,' she said. And I thought, 'Excuse me, I ring you up, I'm about to tell you our marriage is over and you're going to work for a company called Breakmate? You couldn't make it up.'

A couple of weeks after that call I went home and told her, 'Jenny, I'm sorry, this is no good, we're finished.'

'Darling, please don't leave me,' she said, bursting into tears. 'I love you.'

I thought, 'No you don't. What you love is the status quo and you're frightened of what might lie beyond.' I moved out and went to live with a friend and she stayed in the cottage until we sold it – and neither of us looked back. We were both young – I was twenty-eight, she was twenty-four – we had our whole lives ahead of us.

Divorce is a strange thing. However relieved you are to be apart at last, you get waves of sadness because something that was once rather wonderful, that you created together, has now gone irretrievably wrong.

Judy and I weren't living together at the beginning because she had the boys and she was still married, although she'd left her husband. They had sold their house in Barnet and she had bought a flat in Muswell Hill, close to my rooms, so we were seeing each a lot of each other and I was getting to know the children.

As the divorce was getting closer and closer, and papers were zipping backwards and forwards between solicitors, Jenny and I had a warm conversation. I hadn't seen her since we'd parted so we agreed to meet again. Judy later told me that when I left her flat saying, 'I'm going to talk things through with Jenny again,' she thought that would be the last time she'd ever see me. To be honest, at that moment I probably thought the same, that I was willing to give it one more try because we still had the house and I thought that, perhaps, the relationship wasn't beyond repair.

On my way to meet Jenny, I called in to see my former

landlady, Lishy, and poured the whole story out to her and told her what I was planning to do.

Lishy listened, then she looked at me and said, 'Charles, don't do it. Get in the car and drive back to Judy.' And it was the most wonderful piece of advice. I didn't see Jenny that night and I've never seen her again.

So thank you, Lishy. Wise, wise woman.

In 1991, there was an article in the *Daily Mail* that traced some of the girls who had their engagement photographs in *Country Life* twenty-five years before. Because Jenny had been been one of them, they tracked her down and interviewed her. The piece read, 'She soaks up the sun by the pool next to her villa on the southern Spanish coast; down in the harbour is her boyfriend's fifty-foot yacht.'

It went on, 'Twenty-five years ago, when she posed for her graceful portrait in *Country Life* she was engaged to actor Charles Collingwood, who was older than her.' Then there was a quote from Jenny, which read, 'My father had owned an iron foundry in the Midlands and he wasn't too pleased when his only daughter got engaged to an actor she had met in the South of France and who didn't have much money.' It also read, 'She was the daughter of solid country stock.'

My darling mother, who never said boo to anybody and was the nicest person in the world, was very cross on my behalf. When I called her to talk about it she said, 'I don't think the outskirts of Guildford is solid country stock, do you, darling?'

A wonderfully camp line from my mother and a great footnote to a brief marriage.

FIVE

Stilgoe, Marlowe and Me

The frequent bouts of unemployment during my first marriage were punctuated with the occasional stage job, including three consecutive Christmases, from 1969 to 1971, in the West End production of *Toad of Toad Hall*. I played the front half of the horse (the speaking part!) and the fat policeman, but most of the time I was chasing the ferrets, weasels and stoats – the female ones of course. By then, Richard Goolden had made his name by playing Mole for over thirty years, and he was getting on a bit. Instead of a dressing room, he used the broom cupboard at the side of the stage so that he didn't have to walk too far. He was tiny, and he had his make-up all laid out on a little box in the cupboard. He did his own Mole make-up, which was terribly unsubtle and, over time, he had even made most of his costume. It has to be said, it was pretty smelly, too, because he'd been wearing it for the last thirty years.

To generations of children and adults, Richard *was* Mole and after the play, hordes of the younger ones wanted to meet him. He would have a succession of tiny children parading down to the broom cupboard where he'd give them sweets. Can you imagine, today, a bachelor actor being allowed to invite children down to the broom cupboard by the stage to give them sweets? I don't think so.

Richard was marvellous as Mole but he was well into his seventies and could fall asleep at the click of a finger, which tended to create a problem. In the opening scene, Marigold goes into a dream sequence, which takes her into the story of *Toad of Toad Hall*. This is done in front of the gauze, and behind that is the set of the riverbank, where Toad, Mole, Ratty and Badger are gradually discovered. Mole begins the play lying under a big pile of leaves, and as soon as Marigold has finished her dream sequence, up goes the gauze, the music starts and the leaves start flying up one by one as Mole emerges after a long winter of hibernation.

After a week of this, Richard told the stage manager that he was getting a little stiff.

'I'm having to lie out there while Marigold's doing her bit,' he complained. 'Could I possibly have a couple of cushions, because it's beginning to hurt?'

For the next performance, some comfortable cushions were found, he got into position, was covered in leaves and snuggled down. Up went the gauze – and all we could hear was snoring! The band started playing his music, but nothing was coming from the middle of the stage except loud snores, so the cast started shouting 'Dicky! *Richard! Moley!*' and chucking the most appropriate things we could find at him, until suddenly he woke up, but instead of the usual subtle scene, there was an explosion of leaves, like a firework going off and he shot out of the hole! For the rest of the run he was only allowed one cushion.

There's a famous court scene in *Toad of Toad Hall* where Toad is on trial and his friends, Badger, Ratty and Mole turn up to defend him. We all had to learn Mole's lines too because most afternoons Richard fell asleep during the court scene and didn't hear his cue, so we had to step in to keep the thing going.

Gradually, as he got even older he became more inaudible. But there were always two occasions when he gave a really great performance. One was at the start of the second week of rehearsals, when all the young girls playing the animals joined and, because he wanted to impress them, he'd always make sure they heard every word. He also did a trick with a cigarette, which he placed on the end of his tongue and then folded it back into his mouth, before sticking it out again. The girls were so mesmerized by this trick that they didn't watch anybody else. The other time he was truly audible was when the film star Mary Ure was out front. He adored Mary (who was married to the actor Robert Shaw) and, whenever she brought her children to the show, we knew she was in because Richard's voice was twice as loud.

Ten years later, when I joined *Dirty Linen* in the West End, Richard was playing one of the major roles and was still a great character. Before one performance, I arrived early and he was on his own in the green room so we had an hour to kill. I shall never forget this time with Dicky Goolden, because it was one of the most marvellous hours I've ever spent with an actor. First I asked him if he'd ever been on *Desert Island Discs*? He said 'Yes, twice.' And I thought, 'Wow, that's something isn't it? He's had sixteen gramophone records and two luxuries!'

'What about *This is Your Life?*' I asked.

'Yes,' he replied. 'I did *This is Your Life*, but the trouble is I don't have a television and I didn't know who Eamonn Andrews was. So when this man, this stranger, came up to me and said "Richard Goolden, This is Your Life." I said, "Who are you? What do you mean, This is Your Life?" Eamonn said, "We want to take you away and tell people on television all about your life" and I asked, "How long is this programme?" When he said half an hour, I said, "You can't possibly do my life in half an hour."!'

Richard had a lifelong fondness for France. Every year since the war, he went to France at the end of June until the autumn.

He told me that would get the boat to Calais, walk out of the town and spend the rest of the summer in various villages with French friends. He was fluent in French, and these were people he'd known all his life.

'What's rather depressing is all those pretty young gels I used to go out with are now dressed head to foot in black, with very few teeth,' he joked.

'What do you mean you walk out of Calais?' I asked him.

'I walk out of Calais to the villages, I find somewhere to stay and put my head down. I've done it all my life.'

'What do you do about clothes?' I asked.

'That's a good question, Charles,' he said. 'I'll tell you. Just outside Calais is a little country lane and in the hedge I've hidden a suitcase, and I've got all my French clothes in there. Every year I go in the clothes that I travel in, I take the suitcase out. I take off the clothes I've been wearing, I unpack the suitcase, put my French clothes on, pack my English clothes in the suitcase and put the suitcase back in the hedge. When I'm going home at the end of the summer, I do the reverse.'

Returning to my time in *Toad of Toad Hall*, quite one of my most embarrassing memories comes from the production of 1971. As I mentioned, I was playing the front half of Alfred the Horse and a reporter from the *Daily Mail* came down to interview me for a feature on pantomime animals. Rather pompously, I told him, 'You really have to be able to act to play the horse,' and the next day, my picture appeared in the *Daily Mail* with a huge headline: 'RADA-trained actor: You Really Have to be Able to Act to Play the Horse'. The following summer, I was at the Marlowe Theatre, Canterbury, playing Rosencrantz in *Rosencrantz and Guildenstern are Dead* and, sending myself up, I told Richard Frost, who was playing Guildenstern, about that *Daily Mail* interview. 'My God!' he said, falling about. 'I don't believe it! It was you! Last year in panto here, we stuck your photo up in the dressing room and everyone was saying, "Who *is* this prat?"'

As well as the fat policeman and the front half of the horse, I understudied Toad. The actor understudying Badger, while also playing Chief Stoat and Mr Turkey, was a young actor and a great friend of mine called Anthony Andrews, and I could sense that he thought the whole thing was rather vulgar. As Mr Turkey he only had to say 'Gobble, gobble', and he didn't often get that right. I actually felt sorry for him because he looked so embarrassed when we did understudy rehearsals. I thought, 'I'm not sure you should be an actor, Anthony.' For a long time it seemed that nobody else thought he should be an actor either because he didn't work much. He had a lovely little flat in Soho and I used to pop in after auditions for various commercials and the like. He'd sit there strumming at his guitar while we drank coffee and I would think, 'He certainly has the looks of a leading man.' Then one day, I turned on my television and there was a programme called *Danger UXB*, where a young subaltern was defusing mines, and it was my mate Anthony. Shortly after that he picked up a part in a little TV production called *Brideshead Revisited* ...

Anthony has had the most stonking career as a 'lens actor', and maybe at that time he thought big performances on stage were rather vulgar, but by God when the lens discovered him, he knew exactly how to act. Judy's famous cousin, the *Doctor Who* star Patrick Troughton, always described acting on stage as 'shouting in the evenings', which is very apt. Some actors are just more comfortable when there's no need to project. Mind you, Anthony has learned the art since. Judy and I went to see him playing Henry Higgins in *My Fair Lady* at Drury Lane and he not only played the part brilliantly, but sang it beautifully too.

How I admire the way he made that progression from Chief Stoat and saying 'Gobble, gobble' as Mr Turkey to international stardom. Perhaps, even then, he knew that you don't become a star by saying 'gobble, gobble' on the West End stage.

In 1970, I was asked to appear in an Easter production at a theatre in Derby and I found digs on a local housing estate. My car at the time was a Triumph Spitfire, of which I was rather proud. As I pulled into the drive of my temporary home, the rather pathetic figure of my new landlord came out of the house and, without so much as a 'Hello' said, 'We've had better cars than that on our driveway.'

Despite his rather dreary lifestyle, my landlord and I did share one memorable night out – memorable to me, at least, because I'd be surprised if he could remember a thing. He told me he liked a drink and invited me to accompany him to the local rugby club stag do. It turned out he couldn't hold his alcohol at all and, after one pint, he fell asleep.

As he slept, the evening took a much more entertaining turn as the inevitable stripper arrived. She came on to the stage, put her music on, and started peeling off her clothes. The men who had arrived early in anticipation, were sitting in a row of chairs at the front of the hall and, when the stripper was stark naked, she came down from the stage and sat on one spectator's lap. As she gyrated on his lap, the delighted man put out a tentative hand towards one of her breasts. Quick as a flash, without changing her routine, she smacked him straight across his face, breaking his glasses and splitting his nose. There was blood everywhere but she carried on as if nothing had happened, finished her act, then she picked up her clothes and went to walk out. I have never seen a crowd of burly rugby players clear a path so quickly. It was like the parting of the Red Sea!

I always thought her reaction was mildly over the top, but

her killer karate chop was impressive nonetheless. Of course, the moment she left the building, my snoozing landlord woke up and asked, 'Has she been on yet?'

In the summer of 1971 I met one of my oldest friends, Richard Stilgoe, for the first time. I was working at the Marlowe Theatre in Canterbury, where David Kelsey was the theatrical director, and I had been booked for four shows in fortnightly repertory; *Hadrian VII*, *Beyond the Fringe*, *Hamlet* and *Rosencrantz and Guildenstern*, in that order. Because of his immense skill as a pianist, Richard Stilgoe was brought in to do the Dudley Moore bits in the famous revue *Beyond the Fringe*. I didn't make a great first impression. We were introduced by David Kelsey.

'Charles Collingwood, this is Richard Stilgoe,'

'Ah,' said I. '*Still going* strong?'

'Oh, well done,' said Richard, giving me a fixed grin. 'You get a prize for being the seven millionth person to have said that!' He was quite right. Not a good start to a friendship.

We enjoyed our time together in *Beyond the Fringe* and found that we shared a love of cricket, so when we had time we would nip up to the St Lawrence ground in Canterbury to watch Kent play. We made each other laugh but we were very competitive: I thought I was funnier than him and he thought he was funnier than me. If you look at the success of his career, he probably won that one.

On arrival in Canterbury, we were told that a director had been brought in specially for *Beyond the Fringe* and his name was Burt Lancaster. Richard and I couldn't believe our luck! How could it be that this famous film star was going to come and direct us? We were thrilled! So we were mildly disappointed when up turned a man we didn't recognize who was only about three feet tall.

Quite soon, we weren't too sure of his ability either because he didn't get off to a good start. For those who don't know, *Beyond the Fringe* begins with three of the cast sitting on the stage reading newspapers, and the pianist, Richard Stilgoe in our case, comes on and plays the National Anthem, at which point the three men on the stage put down their newspapers and stand up. It works brilliantly because the entire audience follows suit, and when it's over, the three men sit down again, as does the audience. Then the pianist goes offstage, there's a ten-second pause and he comes back on and does it again, so the three men stand up once more and this time so do half the audience. It's a very simple gag, but it's terribly funny. Burt Lancaster, for reasons none of us could explain, decided that we would do the American opening, which was 'The Stars and Stripes'. Quite clearly, coming on and playing 'The Stars and Stripes' doesn't have the same effect at the Marlowe Theatre in Canterbury, so Richard and I lost confidence in our new director very early on.

During rehearsals for *Beyond the Fringe* I was in *Hadrian VII*, which is about a fictitious pope. It is very stagey and there are a lot of cardinals, bishops and priests and I was the Bishop of St Albans. Our first entrance, about twenty minutes into the play, was through the foyer, from the back of the theatre, and we would suddenly appear from the back of the stalls and proceed to the stage chanting and swinging the incense, invoking the atmosphere of a cathedral. It was very effective, so every night when our entrance was due, we would go out of the stage door, run round through the car park, go into the foyer and start our procession. On one particular night, Burt Lancaster came to see this production but he was suddenly taken ill in the stalls and fell unconscious. He had to be carried out and laid down on one of the plush seats in the foyer while a doctor was called. This coincided with the moment that we were all rushing through the car park to make our entrance. As we went in through the front of the theatre, we saw him laid out and said, 'My God, poor old Burt. Look at him.' So all of us – dressed up as cardinals and bishops and clergymen, caked in make-up – gathered round the stricken man, staring down at his face. At that moment, with perfect timing, Burt opened his eyes, saw a host of bishops and cardinals, and for a second he thought he'd made heaven – until he saw my ugly mug staring down at him, grinning from ear to ear.

I do hope Burt made a full recovery and I'm sure he did, but the illness turned out to be fortuitous for us because David Kelsey took over as producer of *Beyond the Fringe* and, of course, reinstated the National Anthem.

Although we got along, Richard Stilgoe and I didn't really form a friendship then, perhaps because of our competitive streaks, but I admired him immensely. At the end of the production, when he was leaving, I said goodbye to him and, as he disappeared into the distance, I said to the remaining members of the company, 'That guy is so talented that if he doesn't become famous it will be a terrible waste.' Richard always says he's a 'jack-of-all-trades and master of none'. I actually think he's master of an awful lot of things.

Our paths didn't cross again until 1973, when I was asked to do a revue called *Good Edgar* at the Bath Festival. When I was told it was written by Richard Stilgoe I said, 'Well he won't want me. We were such rivals when we were working together before.'

'Actually, he's asked for you,' I was told. Richard wrote this marvellous revue, which we performed with Patricia Michael and Cyril Fletcher's daughter, Jill. Cyril Fletcher came one night and treated Richard and I to a lecture on how to be funny. We didn't feel we learnt much from him that night, but we were cocky young pups, who thought we knew everything about comedy. John Baddeley, who played PC Drury in *The Archers*, was also in the show. John is one of the funniest men I've ever known, one of those people you just look at and start to laugh. Richard wrote a duet that John and I had to sing, face to face. After about three days, I insisted we sing it back to back because otherwise I could never have got it out.

Two characters in the show were Bartholomew and Sage (basically Morecambe and Wise), and the routine included a duet called 'Rape and Pillage'. I was playing Eric Morecambe (Bartholomew) to Richard's Ernie Wise (Sage), and I knew the most important prop for me was the glasses. I felt sure that if I could find the right glasses I would be able to mimic Eric, so I walked round Bath searching all the opticians until I found the frame that was absolutely Eric Morecambe.

Just as Ernie always came on first and Eric would sidle on from the back, I would be coming on behind Richard and sidling up behind him. On the first night, glasses on, as I came round the curtain thinking, 'God, I hope this works,' the audience burst into applause even before I'd opened my mouth. 'Yes!' I thought 'Got that one right.'

The right props can so often have an influence on an actor's performance. A fellow student at RADA was Nigel Lambert, who is one of the lippiest, funniest people I know. Shortly after we left RADA, Nigel had a very small part in a West End production that starred Paul Schofield. This was the scene: the curtain went up, there was the interior of a pub and Nigel, playing a very elderly innkeeper, was cleaning the tables. The wind was blowing outside, there was a bang on the door, he crossed to the door, opened it and Paul Schofield, the star, entered with a group of friends who needed rooms for the night. Nigel was just the innkeeper in Act 1, but even at that age, straight out of drama school with a tiny part, he couldn't stop giving his fellow actors the lip and taking the mickey.

During the rehearsals he had been struggling to find a character for the old innkeeper. He was only in his twenties, and the director kept saying, 'Nigel, you're just not convincing me. You're not making him old enough.' He tried everything until he fell upon an idea, 'I know, I'll wear pince-nez, stick them on the end of my nose, with a little bit of string round my neck.'

Relaying this tale to me years later, he said, 'It's funny, but as soon as I put them on I felt I was an old man. I got the walk, I got the voice, I got everything, all because of these pince-nez.' Rehearsals went well but, all the while, he was still letting his mouth run away with him, particularly with Paul Schofield.

Opening night in the West End arrives, and at curtain-up Nigel, as directed, is cleaning the tables, wiping the surfaces down, the wind's blowing, when there's a bang on the door. 'I'm coming, I'm coming,' says Nigel, as he shuffles across like a little old man. He opens the door, and Paul Schofield walks in to rapturous applause. From underneath his cloak Paul produces a pair of scissors and deftly cuts the string off the pince-nez, puts the scissors back and carries on. So Nigel, my cocky young friend, is left with a pair of pince-nez on his nose and the string dangling unattached round his neck. Brilliant! And even more brilliant that Nigel was able to tell it himself.

The fortnight in Bath cemented my friendship with Richard. The revue didn't start until ten o'clock each evening, so during the day we would all go off in his huge Daimler, consume large lunches and then sleep in the afternoon. After the show, it was drinks and sandwiches in the bar until they chucked us out. One night, Richard invited us all to go back to his room to carry on drinking and said, 'Give me five minutes, it's a bit untidy, I'll go up and sort it out.' So we finished our drinks and a quarter of an hour later we went up to his room. The door was open so we went in and we could hear him shouting, 'Help! Help!' We were on the seventh floor and he was outside, clinging to the windowsill by his fingertips. We raced across the room, thinking he was about to plunge 200 feet to his death – and the bugger was standing on a fire escape just below the window.

Another incident, which I find less easy to forgive, was the morning that room service banged on my door at 4.30 shouting, 'Room service! Room service! Breakfast, sir.' Richard had filled in the form and hung it on the back of my door before he'd gone to bed and ordered me the full English breakfast.

To my great joy, when he married his second wife, Annabel, he invited me to be his best man. Actually, he's the one person I know who doesn't need a best man because he can do everything himself, but I did my utmost, and we've remained truly good friends ever since. When I appeared on *This is Your Life*, he paid a charming tribute; 'Because he's played Brian all these years, what many people don't know is that Charles is one of the funniest actors we've ever had and it's a shame you haven't seen him do it.' A generous sentiment; you're only as good as the script, and when you do comedy shows with Richard Stilgoe, you're not dealing with rubbish.

We have worked together many times since, including on his Radio 4 series *Stilgoe's Around ...*' with Belinda Lang, later of *Two Point Four Children*, and the brilliant American actor Kerry Shale. The producer, David Roper, had the great idea that we would go all round the country, exploring different themes, so there was a *Stilgoe's Around on Defence*, *Stilgoe's Around on Industry* and so on. We'd then do the show *in situ*, so, for Defence, we did it on an aircraft carrier. When it was on Industry we played the Elastoplast factory owned by Smith and Nephew in Hull, recording in the works' canteen during their

ABOVE: Calcutta around 1920. Grandpa at the wheel; proud son, my father, at his side; nervous chauffeur at the rear!

ABOVE: Richard and Amy Atherton, my mother's parents. Sadly, I never knew my grandfather, and only just remember my grandmother.

RIGHT: A contribution to the war effort. My proud parents Jack and Molly at Penfield Ridge, New Brunswick, Canada.

TOP LEFT: Walberswick, Suffolk, 1950. Happy parents, but bitter wind, freezing water, stinging jellyfish and sand in sarnies made me appreciate West Wittering, Sussex, all the more!

ABOVE: Aged seven, about to start prep school. How could they send such an angel away?

LEFT: Rosemary Cottage, Amport, summer 1957 (top). Disaster struck on Whit Sunday in 1958 (centre), but twelve months later the cottage was rebuilt – so different but still in keeping.

ABOVE: Can you spot me? A clue: I'm standing on the right – in a dress. What would the Admiral have had to say?

LEFT: Capt 1st XI, St Neots Preparatory School, 1957, with my parents and our beloved dog Damson.

BELOW: House play at Sherborne, I'm in the DJ at the front. The chap in the glasses, also sitting, is Johnnie Watherston, who rose to great heights in BBC TV Sport. The chap behind him rose to even greater heights in the theatre: Sir Richard Eyre – never gave me a job. Probably wise!

ABOVE: 'Dancing' with Polly James in a RADA musical called *Once Upon a Time*. All I remember about this production was I had a huge zit, which made me very self-conscious and added little to my performance.

BELOW: An early publicity photo as an actor. Sorry I had to grow older, Judy! (*Frazer Wood*)

BELOW: Cedric in BBC TV's *The Raven and the Cross*, pretending to play the lyre. Convinced?

BELOW: Just engaged to my first wife, Jenny. Neither of us look too sure!

BELOW: *Letters from an Eastern Front,* Hampstead Theatre, 1966. *(John Vere Brown)*

ABOVE: My God, but you're lovely.

BELOW: With Jackie Clarke in mock Noël Coward sketch for BBC Schools TV *Mathshow* series.

RIGHT: *Dirty Linen*, Arts Theatre, London, 1979. I played Cocklebury-Smythe, a devious, lustful Tory MP. Why did I keep getting these parts?

BELOW, RIGHT: Early days as Brian in *The Archers* – I think I must have needed the loo! *(© BBC)*

BELOW: Irresistible!

TOP LEFT: Wood Green Register Office, 13 November 1976, Our wedding day. Judy and I were the only English-speaking people getting married that day – the rest were Greek-Cypriots! Please note the lovely Triumph Stag at Judy's side – where is it now?

TOP RIGHT: Darling Lishy, without whose wise and constant advice I might have made a mess of my life, seen here well into her nineties. Taken in Co. Kerry, Ireland.

ABOVE LEFT: What a joy they were to me. Barney (left) and Toby at home in Muswell Hill.

LEFT: A bit corny, but I love this photo, taken outside our lovely beach hut at West Wittering.

ABOVE: Brian, Jennifer (Angela Piper), Debbie (Tamsin Grieg) and Roger Travers-Macy (Peter Haroon). Tense days at Home Farm … when Brian wasn't the only one to be unfaithful. *(© BBC)*

BELOW: A recent photo of the Aldridges, minus Kate. Debbie (Tamsin Grieg), Brian, Jennifer (Angela Piper), Alice (Holly Chapman), with Adam (Andrew Wincott) at the rear. *(© BBC)*

lunch hour. With all due respect to the people who have lunch in the works' canteen at the Elastoplast factory in Hull, they're not your typical Radio 4 audience, and there they were, eating their sandwiches and this middle-class group were doing a half-hour comedy, which was witty, but perhaps not exactly their thing. In the middle of the show we'd have a musical entertainment, and on this occasion they were harpists called The Pheasant Pluckers. Two terribly earnest ladies were plucking these great instruments in the middle of this canteen, and you should have seen the look on the faces of the audience. As they played, I wrote a note on my script to Belinda Lang, 'These two are killing the show stone dead'. And she took it from me, crossed out 'are' and wrote 'have'.

It wasn't their fault, it's just that the harp is not the most sought-after instrument in a factory canteen. The trouble for me was that when we started again, our first sketch contained my funniest line and I was determined to get a belting laugh at all costs for the radio recording. So I did a very naughty thing. We started the sketch as normal but, without telling anybody, I craftily undid the top of my trousers so they were loose and held them up with my left hand. Just as I delivered the punchline I let them go, my trousers fell to my ankles and the room erupted in laughter. Of course, the audience at home thought they were laughing at my perfect delivery!

Fans of *The Archers* will remember Simon Pemberton, who was a real bounder. He behaved extremely badly: he hit Shula; he beat Debbie; and, in 1997, he had to leave the village in a hurry – and Brian Aldridge had the last word. As Pemberton shot off down the Home Farm drive I, playing Brian, shouted out after him, 'I'll get you for this, Pemberton! I'll get you for this!' Not Shakespeare, I know, but it was written in the script and I did it with all the energy I could muster.

When I got home there was a message on the answer machine from Richard Stilgoe, which said, 'Very few actors get the chance to speak such prose to the nation, but you did it with your usual aplomb. All the best, Richard.'

He later told me that he and Brian Sewell had been talking about the line and they came to the conclusion that we all use clichés when we're cornered.

'Absolutely,' said Brian, in his distinctive nasal tones. 'The other day I was driving up the Harrow Road and I saw a large boy beating up a small boy. And I got out of the car and said, "Now, look here. Pack it in!" I haven't said, "pack it in" for forty years!'

Anyway, a week after Simon's on-air departure, I was taking my elderly mother to see Richard Stilgoe and Peter Skellern in their show in Salisbury. Richard rang me and said, 'Will you do me a favour? When I give the cue, will you shout out those words that you said to Simon Pemberton last week?' We'd worked together so much that I trusted him and said I'd do it. Come the night, I was driving my frail old mother to Salisbury to see the show and I thought I'd better warn her because, I felt, if I suddenly stood up in the dark and started shouting, anything might happen.

'Mother, I may have to stand up at the start of the show and shout out,' I told her. 'And I don't want to surprise you.'

'My dear,' she said. 'Nothing you do now ever surprises me!'

We got to the Civic Hall, took our seats in row H and the lights went down. Richard and Peter played a couple of brilliant numbers and I thought, 'Good, he's forgotten.'

Then, all of a sudden, Richard came forward and asked, 'Anyone in the audience listen to *The Archers*?'

I'm delighted to say there was a very healthy 'Mmmm'.

'One of my oldest friends plays a major character in the show and he's in the audience tonight,' Richard announced. 'But I'm not going to tell you who it is. I'm going to let him reveal himself to you in his own way.' Then he sort of peered forward into the dark.

So, taking my cue, I stood up and I turned and I shouted, 'I'll get you for this, Pemberton! I'll get you for this!'

And a thousand people stood up and roared, 'Yeah!'

SIX

Judy . . .

I don't know why, but when I was young I was convinced I should never marry an actress. Two egos under one roof seemed a recipe for disaster. All that fighting for the limelight, darling!

What tosh. The moment Judy and I became an item I realized that, for me, being married to an actress was the ideal. Besides, in our house there's only one ego!

Quiet seriously though, we have tried – and for the most part succeeded – to support and encourage each other when needed. The constant insecurities of our lives make it necessary to understand each other. In fact, there was more than a grain of truth when my first wife Jenny said in her *Country Life* article, 'When he was working things were fine but when he was out of work, then it wasn't so good.' However talented an actor may be, to survive he or she has to develop a protective shell, and be prepared for a lifetime of rejection. However successful, the word every actor hears most during their career is 'no'.

Actors also tend to be self-obsessed: to concentrate on themselves, their appearance, their figure, their voice, etc. Fair enough too, as they have nothing to sell but themselves and, quite understandably, this can make them more edgy and more sensitive to criticism of any kind. To us, 'What about me, darling?' is the norm, but it can become tiresome to those outside the profession.

In 1972, Judy and I were getting to know each other. Also in 1972, Peter Skellern wrote a song called 'You're a Lady' – so it's all his fault! The more we heard it, the closer it drew us together. It just became 'our song' and the timing was perfect. To the two of us it was quite simply the most beautiful song we'd ever heard. Peter's voice, his piano playing, the brass band and the heavenly choir – well, it was all too much. We did try to be good but every time we vowed to go our separate ways and behave like grown-ups, this wretched song would come on and we'd be back to square one, wrapping ourselves around each other and promising eternal love. We just couldn't help it. 'Let's face it,' I thought. 'It's in the title: Judy's a lady, I'm a man, so frankly the rest of the world would just *have* to understand.'

Actually, we became Peter Skellern groupies. We would go to all his concerts and say things like, 'Do you think that's his wife over there?' Pathetic, but we thought he was just wonderful. On one occasion we were driving down to stay with Richard Stilgoe and his wife, when we heard Peter Skellern on Richard's radio show and, greatly daring, we decided to ask Richard what Peter was like.

'He's lovely,' said Richard. 'He only lives down the road with his wife and family. Would you like to meet him?'

Would we like to meet him? We hardly slept that night we were so excited!

The following day, Peter and his wife came over and, for some reason, Peter was sitting on the floor and we were sitting on the sofa. I went over to get a drink and I found myself saying to him, 'What's it like to write a hit record?' I wish I hadn't. As I crossed the room I heard a sickening crunch – I'd trodden on his left hand. Can you just imagine being a fan and then treading on the hand of a concert pianist? I was mortified.

Luckily, he forgave me (I think) and for many years now,

Peter and Diana, Dickey and Annabel and Judy and I have all remained enormous friends.

After Lishy stopped me from making a huge mistake and going back to Jenny, Judy and I carried on seeing each other and we both got divorced. We became a proper couple in about 1974, when Judy bought a garden flat in Muswell Hill and together we created a home. With Judy came a package, her two lovely boys, Toby and Barney, who were seven and five. I have always been a child at heart, so I was only too happy to become an instant dad, and we got on famously. It wasn't always easy because their own father was still on the scene and they would visit him once a month or whenever it was organized, but we got through.

My parents were quite apprehensive when I told them about Judy. After my first wife, who was twin-set and pearls and probably everything they really wanted their little boy to marry, Judy was a contrast. When I told them, 'I think I've fallen in love with an actress,' they just said, 'Oh how lovely darling. Is she out of work too?' When I told them she was in *The Archers,* they said, 'Oh, that's nice.' When I told them, 'The thing is she does have two little boys,' their faces fell; perhaps it wasn't quite what they had in mind so, with fingers crossed, I took her down to meet them.

Judy looked like a little elf at the time. The first evening there my father was taking us out for dinner; down the stairs came Judy, in a full-length Laura Ashley dress, looking like a very, very pretty, slightly hippy elf. My father had never seen anybody like that in his life before. It didn't matter, my parents grew to love Judy. The only problem was that my father did have a tendency to call her Jenny, which as you know, was the name of my first wife, but he would always correct himself. He would say, 'Can I get you a drink, Jenny Judy?'

Judy could always get the better of him. She didn't stand for any nonsense. When my father got rather grand or lazy, or didn't try, Judy wouldn't have it, so in a way I think he developed a slight fear of her – a fear that I share! She hit it off with my mother from the word go because they both loved words and books so their relationship just grew stronger and stronger.

My parents took to the children just as I had, because they were fabulous little boys and such fun. My father, like me, never grew up, so he relished the opportunity to start mending bikes, playing cricket and football and building sandcastles on the beach. Toby and Barney were always doing drawings and cutting things out together, and my parents were always keen to join in, so their relationship was absolutely amazing.

My mother was as wonderful at being a grandmother as she had been a mother, and nothing bothered her. If she put the Sunday joint in the oven and we went for drinks with somebody in their village and stayed too long, it never bothered her. We knew that when we got back the kitchen would be smoke-filled, nobody would be able to see a thing, but there would be a mouth-watering smell and somehow, when it was served up, Molly's Roast, as we called it, was always delicious.

When Judy and I first met, I was involved almost full-time in Schools Television, doing puppet series, presenting, acting and commentaries. It was a wonderful earner because in order to make it pay and make it available to all schools, the programmes were repeated endlessly – and, of course, that meant repeat fees for the actors. In fact, I changed my agent once and went to a splendid lady called Marjorie Armstrong, who looked at my CV and at what I'd been doing and said 'Remarkable, dear! You must be the highest paid unknown actor in Equity!' She might have been right.

The thing that really caught on was *Look and Read* and they created this little character called Wordy, who was a legless little creature that used to bounce around the screen, teaching people about magic E's (when that sounded more innocent than it does now) and double S's. One website described it recently as 'a strange camp orange blob with arms', which sums it up nicely. Anyway, the BBC needed somebody to voice it, and because I was always there at Schools Television, they said 'Charles, can you think of a voice for this little character?'

Now, years before, Hugh Lloyd and I were in a musical called *The Stationmaster's Daughter*, at the Yvonne Arnaud Theatre in Guildford. Hugh was then best known for *Hugh and I* his comedy series with Terry Scott. In the musical, I was one of a singing quartet of City gents. In the last scene, we would all line up onstage in a V shape and stand motionless, as the singer Rose Hill did her ten-minute spot number. One April evening, when we were in the midst of a freak heatwave and the theatre heating hadn't been turned off, I felt a bit dizzy.

'Oh shit,' I thought. 'I'm going to faint.' I pinched my leg, and bit my cheek and I felt all right, and then it was over. I went back to London and thought no more of it until the following night when I got to the same point again. I thought, 'This is where I felt a bit faint last night.' And I started to feel faint again. After about the third time this happened I remember approaching Hugh Lloyd, who was the star of the show, while I was a young, inexperienced actor. He was in the bar because he always liked to have a gin before he went on: he didn't like to 'go on alone' as they call it.

'Excuse me, Hugh. Could I have a word?' I asked.

'What is it, Charles?

'You know that bit at the end when we're all lined up and

Rose Hill's singing her spot number? Well for the last three nights I've felt I'm going to faint. What do you think I should do?'

'Well,' he said without a pause. 'If you think you'll get a laugh, faint!'

So that night, when we got to the point when Rose began to sing, I caught him staring at me, eyebrows raised, and I was trying so hard not to laugh that I forgot about fainting. After that we became mates, and on the last night he said, 'Terry and I are doing cabaret nearby, why don't you come and we'll have a drink afterwards.' Of course, I said 'yes' and on the way I told him a true story about Noël Coward, when he was very young and staying with Laurence Olivier in Brighton. Noël Coward was having breakfast on the balcony overlooking the sea, and as he was buttering his toast, little Tarquin, Olivier's son, ran out and said 'Uncle Noël, Uncle Noël,' then, looking down the street, pointing with his finger, he said, 'Why has that dog there got its front legs up on the back of that dog there?' Noël Coward turned to him and replied, 'Well, you see, the one in front is blind, and the one behind is pushing it to St Dunstan's.'

When I told this story to Hugh he laughed so much he had to pull off the road. When he'd composed himself, he said, 'You must tell Terry.'

After the show, when we were having a drink, Hugh said, 'Tell Terry that story.' Being in the presence of the famous Terry Scott, I wasn't going to get it wrong, so I told it as well as I've ever told it.

The minute I finished, Terry completely ignored me and just said, 'Hugh, where are we doing our show tomorrow night?' He cut me stone dead.

'Right,' I thought. 'I'll remember that.' So, years later when they asked me if I could find a voice for this character Wordy,

I remembered the little boy's voice that Terry Scott had done on a record called *My Brother* and I thought, 'I know, I'll nick it.' So I did, and everyone loved it. So really I have Terry Scott to thank for ignoring my joke all those years before.

Wordy continued to be a part of my life long after I joined *The Archers*. Judy and I once did a personal appearance as Brian and Shula for the BBC at the Ideal Home Exhibition, and we did a morning session with the DJ on stage. There was an audience of a few hundred people and they were loving it because they were all *Archers'* fans. In the afternoon, we came back for another show and this time the audience were predominantly children. You sort of felt the parents had said, 'Go and watch the show whatever it is, because Dad and I are going to look at cookers.'

We'd done about five minutes of *Archers* questions and I could see we were dying on our feet. They were bored, I was bored, and the DJ was hopeless, so I said 'Can I talk about something else?' and went into Wordy mode: 'Ha, ha, ha. Hello Word watchers! Anybody here know who Wordy is?' The whole place went wild, they were all screaming 'Wordy! Wordy!'. I do feel quite responsible because Wordy, after all, was supposed to teach the nation to read and write. Sadly we have a nation that can't read and write, so it's actually my fault.

Wordy paid me a fortune over a period of nearly twenty years, and I'm immensely grateful, because it wasn't very hard work. I used to go into the studio for about a couple of weeks a year, do ten shows and they'd be repeated *ad infinitum*.

Years later, when Judy and I were living in Muswell Hill, the *Radio Times* did a feature on us and used a photograph of us in our swimming pool. Shortly afterwards, at a party, Michael Green, the then head of Radio 4, came up to me and joked, 'Charles, I didn't know we paid you enough money to have a swimming pool.'

'You don't,' I laughed. 'You pay for the chemicals – *Wordy* paid for the swimming pool!'

Just to bring Wordy more up-to-date, in 2002, I was in a TV film called *White Teeth*, based on the Zadie Smith novel, and I was playing someone who was frightfully well-to-do – a bit like Brian in vision. The scene began with me making love to a young Jamaican girl. I'd never made love on screen before and, with a bit of luck, I never shall again. We had to do about twelve takes because, in filming, the sound's never right, the lighting's never right, and all that. In one of the breaks this lovely actress and I were talking about the other work we'd done, and I mentioned that years before I'd been this character in *Look and Read*.

'You weren't!' she said. 'Do the voice then.'

'Ha, ha, my name's Wordy!'

She looked at me in amazement. 'I can't believe it!' she said. 'I loved you at school. My friends and I were Wordy groupies.'

With that, we were called back on set to begin making love again. After the call of action, we'd been at it about six seconds and she looked up at me and said, 'I never thought I'd be shagged by Wordy!'

My father always used to say, 'It's not what you know, it's who you know'. In 1974, the person I knew best was Judy Bennett, and if I'd not known her and been dating her, I'd never have been in *The Archers*, it's as simple as that.

When I met her, Judy was one of the most sought-after actresses playing children in BBC radio. She could play all types of children: boys, girls, American, South African – you name it, Judy played it. In *The Archers*, she even played Elizabeth and Kenton when they were little, and Adam Macy until his voice broke. When they were casting the twelve-year-old Shula Archer, the cry went up, 'Who should play Shula?' and someone said 'Judy Bennett.' She's so talented – I hate her!

In the early stages of our relationship, I accompanied Judy to a party and met Tony Shryane, the then producer of *The Archers*. I told him I loved the programme, which was true, I wasn't being a creep.

'Well, you ought to be in it sometime,' he said and I thought, 'That would be nice.'

The next thing I knew, I was cast to play the part of Dave Escott, a dodgy paint salesman. It was a six-month contract and I had a great time, but it went very quickly. On my last studio day I was having lunch with Tony.

'I'm sorry you're going, Charles,' he said.

'Well, I'm pretty sorry too,' I told him.

'Don't worry,' he replied. 'We'll get you back on a more permanent basis soon.'

'And pigs might fly,' I thought. But sure enough, a few weeks later, Judy came back from recording in Birmingham and said, 'You've got to ring Tony Shryane in the morning because you're going to play a character called Brian, a new farmer, and the rumour is you're going to marry Jennifer.'

'*Yes!*' I thought. 'I'm determined to grab that with both hands,' so I rang Tony and he confirmed that yes indeed, they wanted me to play Brian Aldridge.

Looking back on it, I think now that, unbeknown to me, Dave Escott was a six-month audition for the part of Brian. They must have been watching me all the time to see how I'd fit in, not just vocally, but as an actor, as part of a team, because when you join a cast such as ours, there's no point having some great prima donna who's always going to be late or has a drink problem. Ideally, you've got to find somebody who fits in with the others because you're going to be there for a long time, if you're lucky. In my case, I've been lucky, and here I am, thirty-four years later, playing this wonderful part with all that it's brought me, not least – in fact most of all – a wonderful marriage to lovely Judy.

SEVEN

Half a Household Name

Anumber of years ago, because of my interest in complementary medicine I was asked to help launch a health centre in Hereford. It was one of these new surgeries that would have GPs, homeopaths, acupuncturists and chiropodists all under one roof so they could cross-refer to one another. The event was held in the cloisters of Hereford Cathedral. I arrived and, trying to find the right room, got hopelessly lost. Suddenly, I heard voices behind an ancient wooden door, so I thought, 'Ah, it must be in there'. I gave the door a good shove and pushed it open. Bad mistake. It wasn't the best thing to do because I knocked over a trestle table and a blackboard display unit, and quite obviously this door hadn't been opened since 1206!

It was, however, the right room, so having helped to pick everything up, I was introduced to the chairman, a tall, rather imposing Canadian. My host proceeded to tell the chairman who I was and how long I'd played Brian on *The Archers*. The chairman looked down at me and said, 'So you're *half* a household name?'

'Brilliant!' I thought 'That's what I am. Half a household name.'

In March 1975, after my regrettable faux pas with poor old Jack Holloway, and with the pearls of wisdom from Gwen Berryman ringing in my ears, I went into Studio 3, Pebble Mill, Birmingham, to start my life as Brian. Little did I know that for the next thirty to forty years I would be given the opportunity to play the part of a man who became known to five million listeners as the JR of Ambridge. I've had the opportunity to play the father, the philanderer, the broken-hearted; I've been knocked over by Eddie Grundy's cow; survived car crashes and epilepsy; had problems with teenage children – a daughter missing, a gay stepson; and endless storylines that have been so fulfilling to play. And all the while with the dependable and lovely Jennifer, Angela Piper, at my side.

With Jennifer being an Archer, Angie has been in the programme longer than I have, and she's marvellous. She's got a wonderfully distinctive voice, always calls Brian 'Brahn' and she just *is* Jennifer. There are some parts you feel that lots of people could play but I can't ever imagine anybody else in that role, nor would I want anybody else to play it. We've had our ups and downs – Angie's quite feisty and she doesn't roll over – so there have been tensions, but that's rather healthy, like a proper marriage. Once we're in the studio we do feel like a married couple and I hope we sound like one. I'm enormously grateful that Angie plays Jennifer, because we've had a lot of fun over the years and a lot of laughs.

When I first joined the cast, things were very different from the way they are now. Life was much more formal and we were still on the verge of calling people 'Sir'. It was a most exciting time for me but I was there to prove myself and I prayed no one would realize that I had absolutely no radio experience at all, although they probably did. Before I played Dave Escott, I'd never, ever spoken on radio. All these actors had the most wonderful microphone technique and knew how to turn the pages silently, while I was shooting from the hip, doing it for the first time. Anne Cullen, the very glamorous actress who played Carol Tregorran, turned to me early on in my Dave Escott stint, and said, 'You must have done a lot of radio, haven't you, Charles?' I bluffed that one out, but she had probably seen right through me! Still, I must have made a decent enough impression, or they wouldn't have had me back.

All those years ago, some of the older characters, like Walter Gabriel, Mrs Perkins, Tom Forrest and the Larkins, were legends on radio and many of the actors didn't do other work. They were fantastic characters. Bob Arnold, who played Tom Forrest was a folk singer, and he had played the halls, but *The Archers* was his only acting job. George Hart, who played Jethro Larkin, actually wore knee-high lace-up boots!

These old boys were real troupers. They always made it to the studio, no matter how old and frail they were getting. On rare occasions, they'd even be brought in wheelchairs and practically on stretchers, with no visible signs of energy. Many's the occasion when I have thought, 'Good God, he's going to die sitting in that very chair.' But, when required, they'd be wheeled into the studio, the green light would go on and Bingo! Up would come a wonderful performance.

Chris Gittins, who played Walter Gabriel, was a grand old boy with the most extraordinary voice. Nobody really talked like that, but he became a national treasure. When, in his eighties, he eventually got too old to be in the programme and could no longer live at home, we kept in touch and were told, 'He's in a lovely nursing home and he's very happy there.'

By this time he was pretty well bed-ridden, and one sunny day, when he hadn't been out of bed for weeks, he suddenly appeared in the hall of the nursing home, fully clothed, and said to the Matron, 'I'm just going for a little walk in the fresh air.' Matron was thrilled but concerned, so she said, 'Of course. Be careful.'

'I'm only going to go up as far as the gate,' Chris told her.

So he walked up to the gate, which opened onto the pavement at the side of the road. He stood there for some time, chatting to all and sundry. After a while, he returned to the nursing home and said, 'I'm a bit tired now, so I'm just going to go and lie on my bed and have a doze.' 'Would you like a cup of tea?' asked Matron.

'I'd love a cup of tea,' he replied and off he went.

By the time Matron had brought him the tea he had passed away. When I heard this story, I thought, 'What a wonderful way for an actor to go.' He had one final link with his audience, whether or not they knew he was Walter Gabriel. He'd been to see people, because when all's said and done, most actors just want to be loved. It may seem rather pathetic but it's understandable – we crave applause and approval. Of course, we don't always get it.

Margot Boyd, who played Mrs Antrobus and sadly died in May 2008, was one of the great figures of radio drama, but her earlier theatre career was just as impressive. She had been directed by George Bernard Shaw when she was at RADA and worked with Michael Redgrave, Noël Coward, Vivien Leigh and James Stewart. But eventually she found that radio was where she was most comfortable. Comfortable was a way of describing her too. She was a woman of generous proportions – on her own admission her figure was 46–46–46 – but she always had immaculate hair, manicured nails, called everybody 'darling' and loved her whisky.

When Margot joined the programme in 1984, I'd never met her before, but within a few weeks we both shared a twinkle.

'Darling, you have a nice agent, don't you?' she asked me one day.

'Yes, he's very nice,' I said.

'No, darling, when I say nice, I mean *nice*. He's nicely

dressed, and nicely spoken isn't he? Not one of those *vest agents*.'

'Well, since you ask, he is, yes,' I replied.

'Do you think you could possibly put a word in for me?' she said. 'I do need a new agent.'

So I rang my then agent, David Daly, and said 'I think Margot would be a wonderful client for you.' He agreed to see her.

It just so happened that I was going to see him an hour after their first meeting. His office was three floors up above the shops in Old Brompton Road, and I climbed up all these stairs, walked into his office and found David at his desk, in hysterics.

'What's so funny?' I asked.

'Margot. Margot Boyd,' he spluttered, wiping away the tears. 'She came to see me an hour ago and I have to tell you, she appeared at the door, this vast woman, completely out of breath, like an ancient battleship, heaving, gasping for air. When she eventually got in she put her hand out and she said, "Darling, before you say anything, there are two things you need to know. The first one is this. You'll never see me again, and the second one is I don't want to work."'

Two great lines from an actress.

Norman Painting, now well into his eighties, is the only other original cast member who is still with us. Having played Philip Archer for over fifty years, he is now quite frail, but boy, when that light goes on, he is magnificent.

When I joined the cast all that time ago, quite the best writer was Norman Painting no less, whose *nom de plume* was Bruno Milner. I have Norman to thank for his support and encouragement. His microphone technique is masterful, and in my early days he was the one actor I always watched as I tried to come to terms with the demands of radio drama. If only you could see Norman eating a full English breakfast with nothing in his mouth – he deserves an Oscar. I know Judy shares my admiration of him too. What's more, she frequently calls him 'daddy'!

When I started on the programme we recorded four episodes a day at 9.00, 11.15, 2.30 and 4.45. It's changed a little bit over the years, but that's basically the timescale. In 1982, during the visit of Pope John Paul II, Norman came back from Birmingham city centre, where he'd been shopping in between episodes, and told us a wonderful story.

'I've got to tell you the conversation I've just heard between two Brummie ladies in town,' he said, so we sat down and Norman continued. 'The first lady said, "You know that Pope? He's a wonderful man isn't he? He arrived yesterday at Liverpool Airport and he got in that Pope-mobile and paraded through the streets. Then he went to Heaton Park in Manchester where there were 200,000 and he walked out into the middle, he said a little prayer, gave a little blessing, got back in the Pope-mobile, was cheered by them all, went off to York, stood up the whole way, waving to all the cars as he went by. There were 190,000 in York, same thing, said a little prayer, gave a little blessing, got back in the Pope-mobile, down the M4 to Cardiff, 35,000 people there. Once more, said a little prayer, gave a little blessing. He's a wonderful man that Pope because he's not a young man is he?" Her friend had been listening all the time. "You're quite right," she said earnestly. "But you know, it's his wife I feel sorry for."'

Mary Wimbush, who played Julia Pargetter until 2005, died almost as she left the studio. What a wonderful way to go. She was a great character; into her eighties, she smoked, drank and told marvellous stories. She told us she once went to a party when she was in her seventies, clutching a bottle of wine, rang the front doorbell, and the person opening the door saying 'Mary, what are you doing?'

'I've come to the party,' she said.

'But Mary, the party was *last* night,' replied the host. 'And what's more, you were there!'

When she was in her eighties, she was working at Salisbury Rep, but she was also playing Julia in *The Archers*. On recording days, she got the train very early in the morning from Salisbury to Birmingham, had to change trains at Bristol, got the train from Bristol up to Birmingham, recorded *The Archers*, got the train back to Bristol and was on the train from Bristol to Salisbury when she found herself sitting opposite a man who obviously wanted to talk.

'What have you done today?' he asked.

So she told him that she'd got up very early, got the train to Bristol, another from Bristol to Birmingham, done *The Archers*, was now going back to Salisbury where she was due to go on stage for an evening performance. He paused a moment to let that sink in, then said, 'Forgive me for saying this, but are you a great deal younger than you look?'

My favourite Mary story, which may be apocryphal, but people always put it down to her, happened in the great days of the green room at Broadcasting House, when there was a large radio drama company. All these distinguished actors and actresses would sit round in total silence, doing either the *Telegraph* or *The Times* crossword. And in the silence, someone called out 'I'm stuck. 5, 2, 4, 4, and the clue is "sexual deviance inclined to make you deaf"'. Quick as a flash, Mary Wimbush called out 'Prick up your ears!'

In my early days on *The Archers* I sometimes felt a certain hostility from some of the older actors. You could sense that they were thinking, 'Are we going to be sidelined by these young actors?' Fair enough, I suppose. I'd already replaced Jack Holloway!

Their concerns were not unfounded because Tony Shryane was charming but could be ruthless. Two years after I joined, Brian married Jennifer and the show celebrated its silver jubilee with a party up at Pebble Mill. The cameras were there to film it for the television programme *Nationwide*, and Tony had arranged the seating plan for the cast in the shape of a square in order of seniority, so at the top of the square sat Dan and Doris, Phil and Jill and other members of the family. Sitting with them were Christine and Leslie Dunn, who played her *Archers* husband, Paul Johnson. Down the side were the next most important characters, and I was placed with the postman, the farmhands and the various junior characters at the bottom of the square, opposite the seniors.

I remember, with a chilling feeling, the moment when Tony said, in front of the cameras, 'Oh Leslie, would you mind swapping places with Charles?'

So up he got from the first-eleven team and went and sat in my seat with the fourth-eleven and I went up and sat with the inner sanctum. It was like snakes and ladders. I'd thrown the double six and whizzed up the ladder, he'd thrown a four and found himself at the top of the snake and slid all the way down. He looked crestfallen. He didn't know what he'd done or what was coming next.

Later at the party, Tony sought out Leslie and said, 'Sorry about that, old boy, but we're killing you off.' Sure enough, Paul Johnson died in a car crash not long after. Acting can be a ruthless business.

The technology advanced from disc to tape to digital today but, in the seventies, if we fluffed during a scene we would have to go right back to the beginning and start again. Tony could be a hell of a taskmaster.

Just after Brian had bought Home Farm, he decided he wanted a swimming pool, so they cast Steven Hancock as the swimming pool contractor. For years, Steven had been a star in *Coronation Street* as Ernie Bishop, Emily's husband. His character had been murdered so his career in *Corrie* was over. The two of us were recording a scene and every time we got about halfway down the page, Tony would call out, 'Not working, Steven, can you go back to the top?'

This happened several times before Steven, quite naturally, said, 'I'm just trying to give this man some character, something ...' and Tony's finger went down on the key and he said, 'They're not listening to you, Steven, they're only listening to Brian.' Dreadful.

Even the older, more experienced actors felt the wrath of Tony if they were fluffing. Wonderful old Bob Arnold got nervous while we were doing a scene together once and for some reason he just couldn't get it right.

'Go back to the top,' Tony kept saying. 'Back to the top, not working.'

Poor Bob got more and more flustered. I was a young actor and I saw this old man, as he was by then, the script shaking in his hand, getting increasingly tense. Eventually we finished the scene and all was well. But as we left the studio something made me put my arm round him.

'Bob,' I said. 'You know, there's nobody in this programme that's better than you. You are quite sensational.'

This little Oxfordshire face looked up at me and said, 'My dear old boy.' And he called me 'my dear old boy' until his dying day. He also called me Brian – he didn't call me Charles for the last fifteen years of his life.

At the time I joined the cast, Jock Gallagher was Head of

BBC's radio in the Midlands. When Tony Shryane was due to retire a couple of years later, Jock called me into his office. Absolutely out of the blue, he said, 'Charles, we've been thinking about this, and I'd like you to take over from Tony Shryane as the producer of *The Archers*.'

He couldn't have shocked me more if he'd hit me over the head with a shovel.

'Thank you very much,' I replied, and then I went away, thought about it and talked it over with Judy. Although it would have been a great honour and might have given me job security for life, the terrible thing was that I'm a performer and when the green light goes on, I want to be the one that's doing it and not the one giving the orders. So my answer was, 'No, I'm sorry, I'm just going to go on being an actor if you don't mind.' Who knows where that path might have taken me? I may have been head of television by now and riddled with ulcers. It wasn't to be, but I was flattered to have been asked.

In the end, the job went to a whole succession of interim producers before settling with William Smethurst in 1978. He had been a brilliant *Archers'* scriptwriter and had a lot to offer, but he was even more ruthless than Tony. Telling Colin Skipp (Tony Archer) that he had a riveting storyline coming up and then giving him lockjaw! Not kind to a radio actor. Quite funny though! But he was a fine writer and wrote beautifully for the Aldridges and I'm very grateful to him for that.

EIGHT

New Beginnings

Some fifteen years after Judy and I met, I was appearing in an episode of *Hannay*, starring Robert Powell, and after the read-through, the stalwart radio actor Peter Pacey came up to me and said, 'You do realize you were once the most hated man in Equity, don't you?'

'Why?' I asked.

'Because when we were in radio at Broadcasting House, we all fancied Judy like hell. There wasn't a man in the building who didn't fancy Judy Bennett, but she was happily married. Then you came along, nothing to do with radio, from Schools Television and plucked her away from us all. We hated you.'

Tough!

In November 1976, in the very same year that Brian Aldridge wed the recently divorced Jennifer, Judy and I got married. Funny how life mirrors art.

Because we'd both had disastrous marriages before, tempting fate we tried to get married on Friday 13. Unfortunately we couldn't, it was a Saturday, but we decided to go ahead regardless. Now all I needed was a best man.

At the end of May, just as the heatwave of 1976 began, we had taken ourselves off to the mountains of Majorca while the boys were spending half-term week with their father.

'Much as I find you hilariously amusing,' Judy said before we left, 'it would be nice if we could talk to somebody else.'

'Ah,' I thought, 'She's getting used to me now.'

We were staying in a beautiful little hotel on the west coast of Majorca, high up in the lemon groves, and the first morning we came down for breakfast I was tucking into my croissant, coffee and apricot jam, when this huge shadow of a figure towered over me and a deep Mancunian voice said 'Is this seat taken, pal?'

'No,' I said, looking up, and this man, who looked exactly like Les Dawson, proceeded to sit down with his wife and, like a lot of English people on holiday, put their own butter and marmalade on the table, because 'It isn't right, all this foreign food'!

On first impression, I thought they were dreadful. I was being terribly snobbish and judgmental, so I finished my breakfast and fled. It wasn't a particularly nice morning, so we decided to explore the village and it seemed that round every corner lurked this man with his Super 8 film pointing in my direction saying, 'Just act normally, pal. Act as though I'm not taking this.'

As it happened, we were there for my birthday and at about midday Judy and I fell into a bar for a beer. Of course, these two appeared from nowhere and said, 'Do you mind if we join you, pal?'

'We're obviously stuck with these bloody people,' I thought. 'I'm going to go mad.'

We sat down and I reluctantly bought them a drink.

'Look, I want you to know it's actually my birthday,' I said, rather hoping that he'd leave us alone.

'As it's your birthday, pal,' he countered, 'tonight at dinner, you will have a champagne fountain.'

'You put your money where your mouth is and I shall expect it!' I answered, rather challengingly.

That evening, on the stroke of eight o'clock, the waitress

came over and proceeded to put about a dozen champagne glasses, one on top of the other into a great tower. She opened a bottle of Spanish cava, poured it over the top and, when the top glass was full it overflowed into the glass below and that overflowed in the glass below, and it was the most enchanting fountain you've ever seen – until the waitress knocked it over. But that didn't matter.

We weren't to know it, but that was the start of a lifelong friendship.

His name was Frank Mullings and he was one of the most charismatic people I have ever known. People would ask me, 'Do you know any stars?' and I'd say 'Yes, Frank Mullings' because he was always a star to me. You don't have to be famous to be a star in my book.

That birthday night I realized that Frank was one of the most brilliant, self-educated men I had ever met. This granite of the North Country had been a quartermaster sergeant major, played water polo for Cheshire, rugby league for Salford, cricket for Hyde, and he had an encyclopaedic brain.

His wife, Audrey, was so pretty, like a young Bet Lynch. I remember us sitting round the pool the following day, surrounded by the lemon groves. All you could hear were the cicadas and the tinkle of the sheep bells. Staying in the hotel was a heart surgeon, who was rather aloof and chose to sit very much on his own in his dressing gown, facing the sun. On one particular afternoon, it being half-term a number of children rushed down to the pool after lunch. Frank being Frank, and a wonderful swimmer, hit the water like an Exocet missile and those of us by the pool were soaked, including the heart surgeon who pulled his dressing gown closer round him. You could tell he was thinking what a ghastly, frightful, common Northerner.

Judy and I were sitting watching, and after about half an hour, when Frank had entertained and exhausted all the children in the pool with whale noises and shark impressions, battleships and U-boat sinkings, he hauled himself out of the pool, walked over to the heart surgeon and, dripping with water and with a fag hanging from his mouth, he said, 'Have you got a light, pal?'

The poor little man buried himself deeper into his dressing gown and every pore of his body screamed, 'No! No! Go away!' However, such was the power of Frank that the following morning I bumped into the heart surgeon walking along a dusty street by the hotel, and he said to me, 'Have you seen Frank?' I thought he obviously wanted to go in the opposite direction but he added, 'I've just found this fossil, and I know he'll know how old it is and where it came from.'

By the time Frank left, a day or two before us, the whole village, the Spanish and the English and all those in the hotel, hung on his every word. We made all the promises about getting in touch when we got back, and he said, 'Come and stay and I shall pour you the finest gin and tonic in the north of England.'

Frank and Aud had a terraced house, like those in *Coronation Street*, only his was double-fronted, as in the past it had been the cotton manager's house. Frank had knocked through a wall in the dining room, where he had a full saloon bar, with all the bottles on optics on one side, and stools the other side. It's the best bar I've ever been to, because no money ever changed hands, and he did indeed provide us with the finest gin and tonic – or several – in England, while Aud cooked us the most wonderful food.

We invited Frank and Aud down to stay with us that November. Judy and I planned to get married on the Saturday without them knowing. They came on the Friday and we took them to a Greek restaurant in Muswell Hill.

'Frank,' I said, as we sat down. 'Is there anything in particular you want to do tomorrow?'

'No, pal,' he replied. 'We're your guests, we'll do what you like.'

'Well, Judy and I thought we might get married, would you do me the honour of being my best man?' I tell you what, that stopped him talking!

We got married in the registry office in Wood Green, on Saturday, 13 November 1976. The two boys, Barney and Toby, were there and Frank and Aud were our witnesses. There are several things I clearly remember: firstly, the boys were quite bored so they were running up and down the aisles at the back; secondly that Audrey cried the whole way through – and not quietly – while Frank stood there proudly with his chest out; and lastly that Judy fluffed her lines. Anybody who knows or has worked with Judy, knows that is a very rare occurrence, but on this occasion she fluffed. But the thing I will remember most of all was, just before I took my vows of marriage and total fidelity for the rest of my life, the registrar's lady assistant leant across to me and whispered, 'I've been in love with you for the last two years.'

And I said, 'This is not the time to be telling me that. I'm just getting married for God's sake!'

A year after we got married, we moved into a Victorian house in Muswell Hill in north London. From the front it wasn't up to much, and the price was rather more than we felt we could afford, but the previous owners had done it up beautifully. As soon as the front door was opened and I saw the stunning banisters going up to the top of the house, I realized the house was much bigger than I thought and in perfect condition. After being shown round, Judy and I rang up immediately and put in an offer, which was accepted. We were over the moon. This was the first home we had bought together and we just fell in love with it.

Internally the house was better than we could have made it ourselves because the previous owners were both in interior design, and would think nothing of flying to New York to buy wallpaper and furnishings. They had more money than we had, and were much more imaginative.

For all the style inside the house, the garden was a complete tip. It was pokey, bramble-ridden and over-laden with trees, so my first job was to attack that as soon as we moved in. As I stood on the lawn making plans a lady's head popped over the fence from next door.

'Hello,' she said. 'I'm your new neighbour.'

'Hello, I'm Charles,' I answered politely.

'Is your wife into breastfeeding?' she asked.

Toby and Barney were eight and ten at the time, so I was a little taken aback. 'Our boys are a little old for that,' I replied.

'Oh well,' she continued. 'Should she be keen on breastfeeding at all I am the chairperson of the north London La Leche League.'

'Well,' I thought. 'This is fun.' I could sense a certain intensity in this woman, and I'd already noticed that their front window was full of 'Ban the Bomb' stickers and notices about other worthy causes of which I was not necessarily supportive. Her husband later described himself as an armchair communist, so we were never entirely going to sing from the same hymn sheet.

Over the years we grew very fond of them, but on this occasion, having been asked if Judy was into breastfeeding, I thought I would nail it on the head fairly early.

'I must just tell you about us,' I told her. 'I think you ought to know that both my wife and I are alcoholics, so if you need to talk to us, can your try and do it before about half past two in the afternoon, because we tend to fall over after that.'

Looking appalled, she pulled back from the hedge and, chuckling to myself, I went and reported what I'd said to Judy, who was suitably mortified.

Over the following weeks I spent hours in our new garden building huge bonfires and, because a lot of it was done around six o'clock in the evening, I could sense our neighbour thinking, 'My God, he's awash with alcohol, and having all these bonfires. How dangerous!' She soon learned it was just me being silly and Jill and Johnny Iglesias turned out to be the nicest neighbours anybody could ever have.

My sense of humour can get me into terrible trouble and every now and then, particularly after a late evening, I need a placard saying, 'To whom it may concern, I'm very sorry if I upset you, but I didn't mean it!'

On one occasion, Judy and I went to party and in my cups I must have invited a couple round for dinner. However, in the meantime, I'd quite forgotten who they were, or what they looked like. I'd just read about this young *Blue Peter* presenter who had played a great trick while he was a student in Bristol. One lunchtime, in a very crowded pub, in order to get to the bar quickly, he'd arrived with an egg in one hand and handkerchief in the other. As he entered the pub, he faked a huge, stagey sneeze, smashed the egg on his nose, let the yolk and egg white run through his fingertips, and caught it all in his handkerchief. The entire pub recoiled in horror, pulled away from this revolting man, which promptly created a path for him to get straight to the bar, where he ordered two pints of bitter and a packet of crisps. 'What a great gag,' I thought. 'I'd love to try that!'

My moment arrived when the two people I'd invited at the party turned up on the doorstep and I thought to myself, 'Who the hell are you?' I knew I'd invited them for dinner, but they turned out to be rather duller than I remembered. I showed them into the drawing room and asked them if they'd like a drink and they both opted for a glass of sherry. 'It's going to be a long night,' I thought. I poured them out their little sherries and the three of us sat there not knowing what to say. Judy was in the kitchen, stirring the soup, so I went in.

'I've got to liven these two up,' I said. 'I'm going to try the egg trick.'

'I'm not sure that's such a good idea,' she replied, wisely.

'No, no, it'll be fine, it really will. It'll relax us all, break the ice.' So I took a fresh egg out of the egg basket and I took my handkerchief out of my pocket, I walked into the drawing room.

'Do your glasses need topping up?' I asked. At which point, I smashed the egg onto the front of my nose, as hard as I could and then whipped the handkerchief underneath. Well, as you know, I'd never done it before so the first thing I must tell you, dear reader, should you wish to try it, is that you should serrate the egg a little first, because it's bloody painful! I thought I'd broken my nose. What's more, as soon as I smashed it, egg yolk and white fell faster than anything you've ever known – I didn't get my handkerchief anywhere near it – so it was now on my very pale, grey carpet in a huge, snotty blob. Far from relaxing the guests, they were sitting there in horror because their host, who they hardly knew, had simply walked in the drawing room, smashed an egg into the front of his face and left a huge mess on the carpet.

'Oh Christ,' I muttered, and turned and fled into the kitchen.

'It didn't really work, darling.' I said to Judy, who was howling with laughter. 'I think they're rather more tense than they were before.' We managed to get some cloths to wipe up the mess while Judy apologized for my behaviour, and you could hear a pin drop. To this day, I'm ashamed to say, I have absolutely no memory of what happened after that, or even whether they stayed for supper. I probably drank myself into oblivion.

As you may have guessed, I'm an avid fan of the clever practical joke, and there are two that particularly tickle me, although sadly I took no part in either of them. The first was a large group of drama students who got on to a crowded tube train and, without acknowledging each other, sat dotted about the carriage. After a few minutes of the journey, one stood up and started singing, in a very loud voice, 'Oh, what a beautiful morning.' The other passengers sat transfixed, thinking he was some sort of madman but he carried on, 'Oh, what a beautiful day. I've got a wonderful feeling, everything's going my way.'

At which point, fifteen other students stood up and, as a chorus, sang, 'There's a bright golden haze on the meadow...'

I also love the two actors who, very late at night in central London, placed a whole roasted chicken in the bottom of a waste bin on one side of a road and a bottle of champagne in the bin opposite. Next morning, in the middle of the rush hour, the two actors shuffled up dressed as tramps and, watched by queues of commuters at the bus stop, one started rummaging in one bin while the other did the same on the opposite side of the road. The onlookers were stunned to see the first tramp pull out a chicken and the second a bottle, and then stroll off down the road together ripping chunks off the bird and swigging the champagne!

The summer of 1978 was the first time we could afford a really good foreign holiday, so a last-minute booking found us on the Greek island of Poros with the boys. Toby was eleven and Barney was nine, and the four of us had a wonderful holiday.

Somewhere in our relaxed state Judy and I began to warm to the idea that we should have a baby of our own. Within months, Judy was pregnant and our daughter Jane was born at half past seven in the evening on 4 June 1979 at the Royal Free Hospital in Hampstead. And there is a reason that I remember these exact details.

In the early spring of 1979, I was asked whether I would take over a role in the hit production of Tom Stoppard's play *Dirty Linen* at the Arts Theatre in the West End. The play had already been running a few years, and my friend Edward de Souza had been playing the part of Cocklebury-Smythe, a sort of roué Conservative MP. Why they should have thought of me to take over that part I can't imagine. However, I was delighted. I'd done *Rosencrantz and Guildenstern are Dead* before, so I knew Stoppard's work and loved it, and it was a great thrill to play a leading part in the West End. Judy by now was very pregnant, and Shula had been sent to Bangkok (aptly named I felt at the time) for a while so that Judy could rest, but I began rehearsals for *Dirty Linen* and opened at the beginning of May.

It was quite daunting taking over from Teddy de Souza but I was so lucky that he himself was directing me into it. I remember at one rehearsal he was in the stalls and he called out, 'Could you smile a bit more, love?'

'Why?' I asked.

'Darling,' he said. 'You have arguably the finest top set of teeth in the West End of London, we need to see more of them.' They're still not bad, actually, and all my own!

The day I was due to open in the West End, I realized I was less nervous than I've been for similar jobs. It was because Judy was going to have a baby, and in the great scheme of things she had a lot more to be nervous about than I did.

'This is just a job, I've been trained as an actor. It's a funny play, so if I get it half right they're going to laugh,' I said to myself. And I remember gardening in the afternoon before opening that evening, with a feeling of inner calm.

In fact, Toby recently reminded me that, for days before the play, I wandered round the house singing my very own version of the traditional hymn, 'Nearer and Nearer Draws the Time', which went something like this:

> *Nearer and nearer draws the time*
> *The time that shall surely be,*
> *When Cocklebury-Smythe*
> *Which is played by Ted,*
> *Instead will be played by me.*

Teddy, a fine artist as well as a fine actor, painted me a watercolour for good luck and Tom Stoppard, no less, wrote me the most heartening letter after he saw my first performance – not a letter I've thrown away, I have to say. In fact, if ever I need a little boost of confidence, I reread it.

Jane was born a month after I opened. I was playing a lot of cricket at the time and on 4 June I was coaching at North Middlesex Cricket Club, where I was a member. Every Monday evening after school, hundreds of children of all shapes and sizes descended on the club for coaching. At about 6.30 p.m. I'd stop, go home, change and drive into London for curtain up at 8.30. On this particular Monday, I'd no sooner started coaching, when Judy rang the club saying, 'Tell Charles to come at once. My waters have broken!' So I dropped everything and hurried home, where an ambulance had already arrived. Following on in my car, after the ambulance had left for the hospital, I thought, 'I won't have time to come home, I've got to go straight on to the theatre.'

I arrived at the Royal Free in Hampstead at about seven o'clock, by which time Judy was in the birthing suite, so I told the nurse I wanted to go in. I'd always said I didn't want to watch the baby being born, that I couldn't cope, but when it came to it, of course, nothing was going to make me miss that.

'Put one of these over your head,' said the nurse, handing me what looked like a J-cloth.

'She'll laugh,' I said, because I've always looked so stupid in hats. They made me wear it anyway. Judy was in the throes of labour when I walked in but, sure enough, when she saw me she fell about.

Even at birth, Jane had great timing, like Judy, and she didn't waste any time at all. On the stroke of half past seven, out popped this little girl, and I'm ashamed to say that, when they said, 'Mr Collingwood, you've got a lovely little girl,' my first thoughts were, 'Yippee, no school fees.' A terrible thing to think, I know, and as it would turn out, how wrong I was.

As soon as she was born I gave dear Judy a kiss, then said goodbye to the sloppy little creature that had just popped out and got into my car. By now it was about ten to eight. I drove like the clappers down to the Arts Theatre, parked the car, ran into the dressing room declaring, 'I'm a dad! I'm a dad! I've just had a little baby girl.'

I'm sure I did the play faster than ever that evening – and with a smile on my face the whole way through. Afterwards, I jumped in the car and went back to the hospital. There was Judy, resting, and at the end of the bed was a little fish tank with this seven-and-a-half-pound baby lying asleep in it. And that's the quietest Jane has ever been.

The year she was born was one of the most tiring of my career. As well as the play, I was still in *The Archers* – no Bangkok holiday for me – and recording *Look and Read*, plus a number of other TV shows. Going on stage every night constituted a rest. Most of the play was sitting down, so I would think, 'Good, the phone can't ring and nobody can ask me to do anything. All I have to do is the play now.'

The curtain came down just before 10.30, and quite often I would drive to Birmingham in preparation for recording *The Archers* the following morning. On one occasion Judy had been in Birmingham all day recording and had checked into our hotel for the night. We were staying at the Grand Hotel and I left the Arts Theatre, drove up the M1 and got there about quarter to one. Of course, Judy was already in the room when I arrived, but behind the reception desk, chatting to the night porter was Wayne Sleep.

'It's Mr Collingwood,' I said to the receptionist. 'What room am I in?'

They both looked at the register and said, 'You're in room 364.'

'Great,' I said, 'because my wife's there.' And Wayne, in true theatrical fashion, looked at me with a frantic expression on his face and said, 'Oh God, I do hope she's expecting you!'

They were hectic times, although I'm not knocking it because I earned a lot of money, but it was tiring for Judy.

The summer Jane was born was glorious with long, hot evenings. Every actor will tell you that when you're doing a play, it's hard to relax during the day. You can't. You can barely play sport in case you pull a muscle, you must be careful with your voice – you mustn't shout. But once the show's over, your day starts. With a newborn baby to care for Judy was worn out but I'd get back to Muswell Hill around eleven o'clock on these glorious summer nights, and there would be candles lit at the end of the garden, a lovely supper and a bottle of wine. Then we'd fall into bed at half past one, and Jane would wake up at about four o'clock! I really don't know how Judy did it.

Norman Shelley was also in *Dirty Linen* at that point. Norman was a legendary radio actor. He was Dr Watson to Carlton Hobbs's Sherlock Holmes, but was not a man of modesty. When Carlton Hobbs was given the OBE for his part as Holmes, Norman Shelley was heard to remark, 'It was a joint award.' But he was a sweet old boy. He was the first person, other than me, to see Jane after she was born. He just went into the hospital the following day with his arms full of flowers and said to Judy, 'I *was* going to suggest myself as godfather, but maybe I'm a bit long in the tooth.' He left *Dirty Linen* after a short time, which was a blessing really because, truth be told, he'd spent so much time on radio he'd forgotten his theatre technique, and he needed rescuing at times.

During one performance there were just two actors onstage when Norman dried, stone dead. He had a very long speech and he became a gibbering wreck. As luck would have it, playing opposite him that night was the understudy for the other role and, genius that he was, as Norman was muttering 'I don't know where I am, old boy!' the understudy came in with his cue and rescued him. I walked into the bar afterwards and heard Norman say to Teddy, the director, 'I can't work with that young man again, he cut my part.'

No, no, no! Far from cutting his part, he saved his bacon!

Norman had created the part of Colonel Danby in *The Archers* and, like me, had to go backwards and forwards to Birmingham for recordings. After a time he began to get rather frail and when he left *Dirty Linen* he was replaced by Ballard Berkeley – and what a storming performance he gave! Although years apart in age Ballard and I became instant friends, sharing a passion for cricket in particular. I clearly remember saying to William Smethurst, the then producer of *The Archers*, 'If anything happens to Norman Shelley, I know who should take over as Colonel Danby: Ballard Berkeley,' and to my joy that is what happened.

By then, after a lifetime in films and theatre, Ballard had become a national treasure as the major in *Fawlty Towers*. He always said he earned more money in the last fifteen years of his life than at any time before. Funny old game, acting. Fancy earning more money after sixty-five than you did before!

I was in *Dirty Linen* for thirteen months, and it was a marvellous experience. Life in the theatre is full of surprises, and a long run can occasionally lull you into a false sense of security. Night after night, week after week, it's the same, and there's a danger that your mind might wander. It's possible to go through a whole passage of dialogue and then realize that you were actually thinking about going to Ikea tomorrow and picking up a flat pack.

Outside the Arts Theatre were photos of the two male leads, gawking at the beautiful secretary in her underwear, stockings and suspenders. For those who didn't know better, it looked like a peep show and from time to time we would get a few guys who had been drinking all afternoon, thinking it was their kind of entertainment. They were soon disabused of that. Curtain up and Maddie Gotobed, the sexy secretary, came on, lifted up her skirt and took off a pair of knickers, opened a drawer in the desk and, very sexily, exchanged them for another pair of knickers. The louder the reaction from the audience while she was doing this, the more the next ten minutes was likely to be played in total silence because, as soon as she'd put on her knickers and sat down, Alan Hey and I came on and delivered ten minutes of French and Latin quotations. All those who were after something more titillating were very confused.

On one particular occasion, after about four minutes of Latin and French quotations, I looked from behind my *Times* at my co-star, Alan Hey, and said, 'De gustibus non es disputandum,' and a man in the audience shouted out, 'That means fuck off!' which slightly threw me and almost reduced the girl playing Maddie to tears. The cleverer we got with the dialogue, the more noise he made, nearly ruining the play for the audience. The only good thing about drunks is that they go to sleep, and after a short time all we could hear was some rather heavy breathing from Row F – and not the sort of heavy breathing he'd intended, either.

I felt Alan Hey was rather frightened by the size of his part of McTeazle. He also liked a drink, and it worried me that every night, at 7.30 p.m., an hour before the performance, Alan would go to the bar and have two large whiskies. The play ran for an hour and forty minutes, without an interval, and we were offstage for twenty minutes before we came back for the end, during which time he would go to the bar again and have another two large Scotches. After the show, he would go to the bar and have two more before catching his train home. It didn't exactly enhance his performance, but he had obviously been a heavy drinker all his life so he coped with it. The worst nights were matinée nights, because we had an early evening performance at seven o'clock and another at nine, so he would have two large whiskies at 6.15, then again in the twenty minute gap and a further two before the second show, so by the time nine o'clock came he had six Scotches inside him.

One Saturday night, when it was absolutely packed, we went onstage and I didn't like the look of him. He'd had no more than his usual, but that evening I could see added fear in his eyes. We got through the Latin and French quotations and he began a long complicated and witty speech that sets up the play for the rest of the evening. The play is set in a committee room in the House of Commons, and I sat at a table reading *The Times* as he told Miss Gotobed about the committee's duties. He got to about line three and he started saying, 'um'. He said 'um' ten times. The prompter in the corner fed him the line, but he hadn't a clue what came next. Fear had kicked in and so had the alcohol, so he continued going 'um, um, um, um. Um, um, um, um, um, um.'

The audience were rocking with laughter because Tom Stoppard is so original that he might well have written seventy 'ums', but then Alan uttered one 'um' too many and, in an instant, they went pin-droppingly quiet. I could see in the wings that the poor prompter had alerted the company manager, the girl playing Maddie was whimpering quietly in the corner and I was thinking, 'He's had it. Luckily this is the only long speech he's got and if we can get past this we can get on with the play.'

It suddenly occurred to me that, as luck would have it, my next line was, 'Well, this is getting us nowhere,' which indeed it wasn't.

'Well, this is getting us nowhere,' I said, putting down the paper and walking round the table to face Alan. 'Do we have a quorum?'

'What's it got to do with you whether we've got a quorum or not?' he slurred. That was not in the script.

I'm afraid that's when I thought, 'Poo to all this. I'm not getting paid to busk it with a drunk on a Saturday night in the West End.' So I turned my back on the audience and waited for the curtain to drop. It was only then that I became aware of the bedlam behind the set, the frantic whispers of, 'When are we going to go on?' and, 'Well, I'll go on now then. Charles has stopped talking. She's crying ...' In the next moment the door burst open and a young actor entered carrying a rolled umbrella, which he threw at me. Normally I had left the stage at this point, and he was meant to throw the umbrella at Alan, but never mind. I caught the umbrella and found myself going to the door, saying, 'Well I'll leave you to it.' Which I did.

Somehow this young man got Alan through to the next short scene, as I watched from the wings with Keith Smith, the other lead in the play, who was in a terrible state, saying, 'What the hell's going on?'

'He's pissed, old darling,' I explained. 'And we've got to get back on and cover for him.' So on we went and, with the rest of the cast, we got through it. Every now and again Alan would mumble a line, but we didn't care by then. We were just determined to finish the play without any further hiccups from him, literal or otherwise!

Afterwards, in the dressing room, Keith and I gave Alan a bollocking. We were livid, and we wouldn't let him go to the bar.

'Thank you very much,' he replied. 'I shan't be seeing you chaps again. I'm leaving the show, and before I go, may I point out that I don't think any of you are any good in this.' And with that, he went.

Anyway, as you can imagine, the audience had been hugely let down that night and, although it wasn't our fault, we all felt very responsible. Over the weekend, I rang the company manager, Alice Lidderdale, who said, 'It's perfectly all right. The management's been on to him, and told him he can't just resign, to look at his contract and be there on Monday – sober!'

On Monday night a very sheepish actor arrived, trembling with fear because he wasn't allowed his usual two large whiskies. That night, he went on 'alone', as they say, got through it, and never drank again. Not before or during the show anyway. Poor Alan; it was fear that made him drink so much.

The final catastrophe for Alan, which was just as bad in its own way, was in the matinée one Saturday when one of his front teeth, which was crowned, unexpectedly fell out, leaving him with a black spike and a lisp. By this time, I'd been in the play for some months, I was doing *The Archers* and fitting in a lot of television, not to mention the fact that Judy and I had a tiny baby at home too, so I was tired. Just to make things worse, Keith Smith, a wonderful comedy actor who regularly worked with Spike Milligan, was the biggest giggler I've ever known. After Alan's tooth fell out I talked to the company manager between the two shows and pleaded with her to send the understudy on.

'Are you professionals or not?' she asked

'Of course we're professionals,' I answered, 'But you know the setup. Keith's going to howl with laughter, I don't know what will happen next.'

'I think it's disgraceful,' she said. 'I'm not going to send the understudy on. You'll jolly well go on, control yourselves, and play it with the lisp and the black spike.'

So at nine o'clock we started, Alan lisped his way through the French and Latin, and Maddie the secretary started giggling. I scowled at her and to my relief she stopped. Soon after I was off briefly and stood in the wings with Keith, who was getting ready to come on as the Chairman. He asked me what it was like.

'It's all right,' I told him. 'He's just got a tooth missing, that's all. He's lisping a bit and there's a black hole ...'

'It's not funny then?' he asked.

'No, no, not funny at all.' I went back onstage, and a couple of minutes later Keith made his first entrance: he walked onstage and simply burst out laughing. He didn't even say anything, just came on and howled. The minute Alan next opened his mouth, none of us could say a word. To this day I don't know what the audience thought, because I couldn't see further than the tears in my eyes. To make matters worse, Ian Gardiner, the actor who had been cast to take over from Alan was sitting in the audience. It was the most shameful moment of my entire acting career.

People often ask why we call it 'corpsing' – I think it's because you want to die when it's over. You don't go home laughing, you go home with your head in your hands thinking, 'What have I done?'

Sometimes, during a long run, an actor can be beset by gremlins in his head which say, 'Why are you saying these silly words? Why are you pretending to be somebody else?' You try to force these negative thoughts out of your head but if you allow them to take hold, you've had it.

One night about nine months into the run, Keith Smith came on and, for no apparent reason, just couldn't remember a word. It was the first Saturday show, and fortunately by then we all knew his lines and were able to get him through. In the interval between the shows he was shaking and begged, 'Go through it with me, will you?' He had been performing for nine months but, however many times we went over it, he didn't know a bloody word. I told the company manager we had a massive problem and she agreed to put the understudy on.

Keith was grateful, 'Oh, thank you. I'll just go home and …'

'You're not going anywhere,' I interrupted. 'You're going to sit out front and you're going to watch the performance. You're going to watch how bad the understudy is. Hopefully, that'll help you realize just how good you are.'

My amateur psychology worked. On Monday, he came back and, of course, he was terrified, but he knew every word. He soon got his performance back to its brilliant best. Oh those bloody gremlins!

Keith was the most meticulous old bachelor. He lived on his

own, and liked everything very neat and ordered. During the run we shared a dressing room and being rather untidy I tended to leave my few sticks of make-up, a can of Coke, a comb and my script lying about, while he had his make-up in perfect order, arranged on a little towel in front of him. Each evening, before he went onstage, he always put a ten pence piece on his towel and, each evening, during the twenty-minute break, he would make a phone call to a girlfriend.

Disturbingly, for a while, we had a thief in our midst, who was stealing cash from those receiving weekly wage packets in the theatre. It caused great tension among the company and we were all under suspicion until she was finally caught. One night Keith left the room and, just before I went onstage, as a joke I nicked his ten pence piece. When I next went back to the dressing room there was a piece of paper stuck to my mirror which just said, 'Put it back, you thieving bastard!'

After thirteen months in the West End, I'd had enough and Philip Voss took over from me. Some years later, Philip was to make a brief appearance in *The Archers*.

After a year out of the production, when Jane was two, I was in a studio off Baker Street, recording an audio book, when I got a message from Judy. 'Your agent needs to speak to you urgently.' So I rang my agent.

'Darling, terribly short notice, but Henry McGee [Benny Hill's sidekick for years, who was playing Cocklebury-Smythe on the tour of *Dirty Linen*] is having terrible trouble with the dates and can't do the last week of the tour in Oxford. Can you step in?'

While we were speaking, Judy rang again.

'Hang on a minute,' I said. 'Judy's on the other line'

'You're not going to believe this,' she said. 'Jane's done her first poo in the potty!' I thought, 'Which of these calls is more important? The poo, of course. Fantastic!'

'Of course I can do it,' I said, going back to the agent. 'But who's playing the sexy secretary? I've got the first twenty minutes with her. I must know if I can work with her.'

'It's Mandy Rice Davies,' she told me.

'I'll be there in half an hour!' I said.

The following week, I went down to Oxford for rehearsals with Mandy Rice Davies, famed for the part she played in the Profumo affair in the sixties. Actors always write their own biographies in the programme so I thought, 'I must see what Mandy Rice Davies has written about herself.' Her biography began: 'After a spot of bother in 1963 ...'

'Spot of bother?' I thought. 'It might have been a spot of bother to you, dear, but it brought down the entire Tory government!'

Mandy was great, so confident and technically very sound, which was all I needed. After the Profumo affair she had done pretty well for herself; she married an Israeli businessman, opened a string of nightclubs, converted to Judaism and became an Israeli citizen.

One day we were chatting and she asked, 'How many performances of *Dirty Linen* did you do in the West End?'

'Three hundred and fifty or so,' I replied, rather smugly.

'Oh really,' she said. 'I did over six hundred performances of *Move Over Mrs Markham* in Hebrew.'

NINE

Brought To My Knees ...

Being a regular character on *The Archers* is a fantastic job because it allows plenty of time to pursue other work. In fact we only record for six days a month, making four shows a day, so it's a luxurious job in that respect.

I have always loved to diversify and, in the late seventies and early eighties, when time allowed, I spent four years as a part-time BBC World Service newsreader and continuity announcer. I was a 'casual' and slotted in when the regulars went on holiday or were sick, but it all came to an end on one memorable evening.

I was getting a lot of night shifts and I was beginning to think I might have done this long enough, because there are only so many times you want to turn up at Bush House at midnight and work through until eight in the morning. This particular night, at midnight, I was sitting in the green room reading my *Evening Standard* when John Wing, a very distinguished newsreader on the World Service, walked in. He didn't see me, but went to his cubbyhole and, to anybody who cared to hear, he said, 'I pity the poor person who's doing the one o'clock. There's been a coup in Czechoslovakia and they've named the new cabinet.' Then he added, 'And what's more they've named the old one too!'

I had never been in the newsroom so quickly. I spent half an hour trying to get some sense out of those long and complicated names and, thankfully, I did. When I went on air at one o'clock

I got through the story about Czechoslovakia.

What I hadn't had time to do was prepare the other news items, and as I got to the end of this ten-minute broadcast there was a piece on Afghanistan. I had to say 'Asadabad'. Now, it's not a hard word to say but, when you've not seen it before, it can prove a little tricky. On this evening, I said, 'Asadabadabad'. And because I'm competitive, I wasn't going to leave it there. I said, 'Asadabada ... Abadasadafad ...' Not a chance. I could see the clock ticking round so I gulped, 'Now here are the main points again.'

I did Czechoslovakia perfectly but, once again, got stuck on Asadabad. In horror, I saw the clock tick way past where I was supposed to finish and when I had, I very meekly went up to the continuity room. As I opened the door Elizabeth Francis, a very frightening newsreader with half glasses, peered at me and said, 'Not one of your best ones, was it, darling?' That was enough newsreading for me.

At the time, I was still heavily involved with BBC Schools Television and I felt terribly lucky because I was writing, presenting, acting, narrating – you name it, I was doing it. One day I was chatting to an actor, who shall remain nameless, and he asked, in all earnestness, 'Charles, don't you think you're in danger of ruining your career? Doing all those puppet voices on children's TV?'

'What are you doing at the moment?' I asked him.

'Landscape gardening,' he said.

'Well, you're not speaking from a position of great strength, then, are you?' I pointed out.

I made a great many friends at Schools Television, not least with producer Claire Chovil. A true bluestocking, Claire was a very serious woman who loved actors and show business, but she had headmistress written all over her. She'd been educated at Cheltenham Ladies' College and Oxford, had never married and was quite strait-laced. I enjoyed working with her and I was much younger so I imagine that, to her, I appeared to be a free spirit, quite naughty and mischievous, all the things that she'd quite like to have been herself. I made her laugh just by walking in the door sometimes and, because she liked me, she gave me a lot of work.

At that time the offices of Schools Television were located at Villiers House in Ealing, close to where I was living, so it was easy for me to pop in to see her. Claire rang me one day to break some good news.

'I must tell you, Charles. I've just been promoted to the Head of Department,' she gushed. 'It's a really important promotion.'

'That's absolutely fantastic, darling,' I said. 'I'll pop in and congratulate you tomorrow.'

'Absolutely,' she said. 'Come and have lunch.'

Back then, there were no ID cards and security checks at the BBC, you just strolled in. The commissionaires all knew me, and they didn't even need to ring Claire's office to say I had arrived. So the following day, just before lunchtime, I walked into the building and decided, in deference to Miss Chovil and her promotion, I would go into her office on my knees. Outside her office, I got down on my knees and knocked on the door, at the same time bursting through it and scuttling in very quickly like a little dwarf, with my hands in the praying position.

Unfortunately for me, Claire was talking to one of the Directors of the BBC at the time, who'd also come to congratulate her, and the sight of this tiny man barging through the door in the praying position, was too much. I saw Claire physically shake, her knees gave way, and she gave a terrified gasp. The Director just remained standing, presumably thinking, 'Who the hell is this?'

'Oh shit!' I said, and, without getting up, I turned left and scuttled into her secretary's office, slamming the door behind me. Having seen the whole thing, the secretary was by now crying helplessly over her typewriter. But I wasn't laughing. I thought my career was over!

I hid in there until the big boss had gone and Claire came in, looking pale. 'What on earth were you doing?' she asked.

'You know me, darling,' I explained. 'I was so thrilled that you got promoted, I just thought I'd show my respect for you in my own sort of way.' Eventually, we laughed about it, but I'll never forget the look on her face.

I didn't get on so well with all the producers, however. In 1975, I was asked to do a series called *Mathshow*, with Jacqueline Clark and Tony Hughes. It was a thirteen-week series consisting of sketches designed to help children understand graphs, fractions and arithmetic. Unfortunately, I didn't get off on the right foot with the producer, David Roseveare.

'I want you to be in this series,' he told me. 'And it's going to last the best part of a year.' Needless to say I was delighted and accepted the job. As I was leaving, he said, 'I understand your other commitments but we'll fit the filming schedule around *The Archers*. Just do me a favour, would you? When you go up to Birmingham next, could you possibly go and shoot the person who plays Shula, because I can't bear her or the way it's played!'

'I must remember to tell Judy that when I get home,' I said. We never really got on after that.

Legendary children's TV producer Dorothea Brooking was a very important person in my life and gave me my break in children's television. During one of my long spells of 'resting', I got a call from Peter Smith, a contemporary of mine at RADA, who had been on the stage management course.

'How do you fancy being an Italian gypsy in a children's television series?' he asked.

'Enormously,' I replied. 'But if you're casting an Italian gypsy, why cast me?'

'I see your point,' he said. 'But the director, Dorothea Brooking, said to me this morning, "Find me someone who can make me laugh for three weeks in Haslemere," and I thought of you!'

Dorothea duly sent for me. I hadn't worked for six months and this gruff-voiced lady, very thin with short cropped hair, austere glasses and a fag on, greeted me with, 'So, Peter says you can be funny. Is that true?' Imagine how funny I felt then! However, that wonderful woman changed my life when she gave me the part, trusted me and continued to use me in almost everything she did until she retired.

In 1974, Dorothea cast me in *The Raven and the Cross*, a children's drama about King Alfred. I played a rather nervous messenger called Cedric and we spent several weeks filming in the gorgeous Sussex countryside in April and May. By then, I had separated from Jenny, I'd just started seeing Judy, I didn't have a home and I was very unsure where my life was going, but I had a few golden weeks down in East Sussex.

Like all actors playing a principal part, I had my own dresser and he was a 'one off' called Leslie Hallam. Before becoming a dresser, Leslie had run his own hairdressing salon near the Connaught Hotel in London, but he gave it all up when they introduced VAT, 'I can't be doing with that VAT, dear!'

Leslie was one of those wonderful, elderly, caring gay men, who referred to himself as Aunty: 'Aunty'll look after you dear,' he'd say, and what great friends we became. He smoked like a chimney, was thin as a rake and possessed a dangerous acerbic, hilarious sense of humour.

Once, on a night shoot, we were filming around a blazing campfire, discussing a battle plan and, despite the flames, we were frozen. Every time Dorothea yelled 'cut' all the dressers would be there with duffle coats to put round us to keep us warm. I always teased Leslie unmercifully, so when they 'cut' for the umpteenth time, I started clicking my fingers at him. Click, click, went my fingers then click, click, again. No response.

'Excuse me, dresser,' I barked. 'When I go like this and click my fingers, it means I want you.'

Leslie gave me a withering look, stuck two fingers up in a V sign and said, 'And when I go like that, it means I'm not coming.'

We were inseparable. If you get on well with your dresser they'll do anything for you. Leslie would knock on my hotel door in the morning and call out, 'Going down to breakfast, love. What do you want?'

'Two eggs and bacon.' I'd answer.

'It'll be on the table, dear.'

On the other hand, get on the *wrong* side of your dresser, or get too grand, and they won't pick up a pin for you. Hell hath no fury like a dresser scorned.

After the filming was over, I went back to Ladbroke Grove where I was staying with a friend while I sorted out my domestic arrangements. Leslie had a beautiful flat nearby in Notting Hill Gate. He had made quite a lot of money out of his hair salon business and he was kindness itself, always asking me round for supper.

One evening, I took Judy there to meet him. I was very nervous, and I confided in him, 'I think this is the woman I want to spend the rest of my life with.' Judy was young, pretty and cute, and the following day I rang Leslie and asked what he thought of her.

'Darling,' he replied, 'If you want to spend the rest of your life with a sparrow, it's up to you. She's a very sweet, cute little sparrow. Peck away.' Judy's certainly the prettiest sparrow I've ever seen.

Because he'd been a hairdresser, Leslie saved me a fortune in haircuts. 'Your hair needs cutting, dear. Pop into the kitchen, pop your head over the basin, and Auntie will give it a snip.' I went into the kitchen, bent my head over the basin and as he came up behind me, he said, 'Your mother would be worried if she could see you now!'

Dear Leslie. He was a wonderful friend. He's gone now and I miss him.

Apart from offering diversity, acting can also fit in beautifully with family life. When the boys and Jane were young, I didn't have to go to the office every day and for the most part, I was a father at home.

On one occasion I was asked to attend an interview for a new television series about river police, which was to be set in Liverpool. My agent said they wanted me for the part of a police surgeon, so I drove into the centre of London on a lovely summer's day, feeling strangely depressed. As I drove, I began to realize why I had this sinking feeling in my stomach. I was thinking, 'I'm already in *The Archers*, working in Birmingham, which is a fine place to work, but not where I want to live; I want to go back to my family and my house in north London. If I get this part I'm bound to be in Liverpool when I'm not in Birmingham, so I'm never going to be at home, I'm going to be miserable, and I'll probably have masses of affairs because I'm so miserable. Everything will go belly up, my marriage will collapse, my children will hate me and all because I'm stuck in two places so far away from home.'

By the time I was called in to the interview I was certain that I didn't want this part. I was greeted by a panel, including the producer and director, who outlined what would be required of me.

'He's the Chief Constable's best friend,' they told me.

'And he's the police surgeon, isn't he?' I asked. 'But why is he the Chief Constable's best friend?'

'They were at school together.'

'Were they? Which school?'

'They were at grammar school together,' they explained.

'Oh, I'm so sorry,' I heard myself saying. 'I couldn't play the part even if you were kind enough to offer it to me.'

'Why not?' they asked, surprised.

'Because I'm afraid I can't play a grammar school boy. I'm so sorry. Thank you very much for seeing me, but I can't ...' Then I backed my way out of the door, rambling and apologizing, and waving at a totally bemused row of faces. I got in my car and I went home singing, 'Hooray, I don't have to go to Liverpool now, my marriage will survive, I'll still love my wife and my children.' It wasn't a great career move but I've never been ambitious. I just wanted to enjoy myself.

Six months after Jane was born, Judy was back at work and we had a series of childminders, some better than others, who would come and help out when necessary. But I was very happy to be a house husband whenever needs be. I've always been quite good at cooking and putting washing in the machine, not because I'm a hero, but I think when you have a marriage based on equality, and one of you is out earning money, it doesn't take a brain surgeon to put the children's clothes in the machine and have fish fingers for four on the table at five thirty.

One morning, when Jane was still a baby, Judy was out shopping and I had been sitting reading the paper, when I saw a mouse run across the dining-room floor. I sprang into action, called the health people and said, 'I think we've got mice.' So the chap came round, put down a couple of traps and said he would be back in a couple of weeks to check them.

As all parents know, in the month or so after a baby is born a health visitor makes regular visits to check that he or she is feeding well and that the mother is coping. A little time later, on a glorious July day, Jane was in her pram asleep in the garden and Judy and I were sitting with the health visitor who was saying, 'Honestly, this house is perfect, and Jane's doing so well. Goodness me, if every house I visited was like this, I wouldn't have a job,' at which point our cleaner appeared at the back door in the garden and shrilled, 'Mr Collingwood, the rat man's here.' The health visitor looked a little pale and I saw her scribble in her notes. All that glitters ...!

Jane wasn't always an easy baby but Toby and Barney doted on her. I remember watching them and their friends, and thinking, 'Children are so much nicer now than when I was a child.' I wouldn't have cared less about someone's baby sister, but all Toby and Barney's friends used to come back from school and fuss over Jane. They would bounce her on their knees, read her stories – she was spoilt rotten by those boys.

As grown-ups, the three children still have a wonderful relationship, although with Toby living in Buckinghamshire, Jane in London and Barney enjoying an alternative lifestyle in Andalucia, we don't get together as often as we'd all like. But, while they were growing up I remember thinking, 'You two are extraordinary boys!' I wasn't their father, although I tried to be in every respect, but there was no jealousy at all. They were fantastic. I haven't ever had a bad word to say about either of them.

Actually, if there was any trouble it was nearly always Jane that caused it. She was a very sweet little girl but, being the youngest, and after all that spoiling and attention, she could be demanding, a bit wilful. Jane was like the Caribbean weather. You either got a serious tropical thunderstorm or a clear blue sky, but there were very few dull grey days. However, as I said in an article we did for the *Sunday Times*, thunderstorms are rare now, it's mostly blue skies now she's grown up.

Jane was a water baby. The moment we put her in water she loved it, splashing around, kicking her legs and grinning, so at an early age, we took her down to the beginner's pool nearby and found she was more confident in water than she was walking. When she was two and a half, she got her pink badge for swimming a width of the pool with armbands. Her teacher looked down at her and said, 'Well done Jane, you get a pink badge for doing that.'

'I want a blue badge. Want a blue badge,' protested Jane.

'No, you get a blue badge if you swim across without armbands,' explained her teacher.

A defiant Jane tore off one armband, then the other, swam all the way back and said, 'Blue badge!'

As a baby, we'd taken her down to the sea at West Wittering in Sussex, where we'd hired a cottage.

'When you take the child into the sea for the first time,' Judy instructed me, 'you should always take them with their back to the waves, because they don't want the waves breaking over them and salt in their mouths, and they mustn't see how far the water stretches out.'

Cautiously, I took Jane into the water for the first time and she immediately ripped herself round in my arms, faced the sea and let the water gush right over her. She never went backwards into the sea again. I'm happy to say, she became a very strong swimmer in her teenage years and swam for her school.

Luckily for Jane, she inherited her mother's looks and talent, and showed an interest in acting at an early age. In fact, she had a part in *The Archers* when she was ten, playing Emma Carter. But, as we were keen for her to get a proper education and not become a child actress, we would only let them use her during holidays, so it didn't last.

While she was there, though, she played a brilliant trick on us all. She was in the studio recording a scene with Brian Hewlett, who plays Emma's father, Neil Carter. When the scene was over, the light went out and ten-year-old Jane came flouncing out of the studio and in a loud voice, in front of all the cast, said, 'I'm not working with him again, he's no use at all!'

Everybody fell completely silent, dumbfounded. Brian had put her up to it and dared her to say it, and she's not frightened of anything, so she took the bait. She gave them all a shock though. No wonder she grew up to become an actress.

TEN

The JR of Ambridge Gets His Spurs

After nine years of marital bliss I had my first affair. I am referring, of course, to Brian's extra-marital dalliance with Caroline Bone on *The Archers*.

The storyline came as something of a surprise. It started with a character in the pub saying, 'Brian's been up to his old ways again,' which was a huge shock to me – and the entire country. The next thing I knew, Brian and Caroline were having this very steamy affair.

My advice to young actors when joining a soap opera (on the rare occasions anyone ever asks for my advice) is that if you're going to create a character, try to give them an 'attitude' of some sort, as soon as possible. There should always be something in the way you say the lines that's going to make the writer think, 'I didn't know that I meant it like that. How interesting.' The writers will then become more intrigued by your character. If you just say the words, even if it is perfectly professional and believable, the writer isn't going to be stimulated by you.

In the early days of Brian, I tried to add a sort of smoothness, an underlying smokiness, which may have created an element of untrustworthiness and made the writers believe he could be a ruthless philanderer. Brian makes his own pace now, but in those days I tried to introduce something over and above just being a jolly nice husband. So when listeners said, 'Brian was happily married to Jennifer and all of a sudden they made him have the affair with Caroline Bone,' that is true, but maybe there was something in the way I was playing Brian that sowed that seed in the writers' minds.

With all new storylines, actors can never anticipate the effect they might have on the audience but, when the affair with Caroline started, the reaction was amazing. All of a sudden, that was all people were talking about, and it was very exciting. There was a real awareness of Brian, and the listeners were rather startled.

The affair coincided with a show about musical plagiarism, which I did with Richard Stilgoe at the Golders Green Hippodrome, backed by a choir and orchestra. Judy decided to bring Jane, who at that point was six, to watch her daddy be brilliant. It was an early evening performance, and they sat themselves in the front row so that Jane could see me clearly.

Richard Stilgoe walked onstage to tumultuous applause and announced, 'To help me tonight, I have my friend, the actor Charles Collingwood.' I walked on to polite applause as Richard continued, 'What some of you may not know is that when he's wearing his other hat, he's Brian Aldridge in *The Archers*.'

Simultaneously, the whole audience booed and, what's more, so did the whole of the BBC concert orchestra. Poor Jane burst into tears, turned to her mother and, through a gap in her teeth, lisped, 'They often boo daddy at the end, but never before heeth opened hith mouth.'

During that period a few of the cast were also in *The Archers* stage show at the Watermill Theatre in Newbury and, during the interval, we ran a fete, with Morris dancers, music and stalls of various kinds, all being manned by members of the cast who at all times had to remain in character.

My job was running the bottle stall and a stockbroker-type came up, bought some tickets and, nudging me, said out of the corner of his mouth, 'Is Caroline with you?'

'I beg your pardon?' I said.

'Is Caroline with you? Ha, ha, ha,' he laughed, thinking I'd share the joke with him but, I said, in outraged tones, 'If you mean what I think you mean, you'll be hearing from my solicitors on Monday!'

He fled, and I watched him go to the beer tent and join his friends where he told them, 'God, I think he *is* Brian. He didn't crack.' Of course I didn't because I was in character, but it was quite a powerful feeling, behaving as my alter ego in public.

The affair with Caroline, played by the lovely Sara Coward, lasted for a long time and even carried on after Jennifer found out. It was a lot less steamy than the passionate fling with Siobhan in the 1990s, but that was an indication of the times. The whole affair was conducted in restaurants, eating and drinking, and not in the bedroom, so there was precious little heavy breathing. That was all to come later.

Even so, that storyline changed my life because it completely altered the audience's perception of Brian. For nine years, Brian and Jennifer had been very happy. Brian doted on his stepchildren, Debbie and Adam, their own daughter Kate had been born, and really nothing could have been better. They were the ideal wealthy family.

Overnight, William Smethurst changed all that when he decided on Brian's first infidelity, and that set the scene for the rest of his life. He would soon be having a go at his cleaner, Betty Tucker, although she took fright when he suggested they skinny-dipped in the pool. Then there was Mandy Beesborough, a redhead who rode in the local hunt. Brian certainly had a passing fling with her, although it was never on air, sadly.

Brian had always wanted a son of his own. He adores his children and stepchildren, but Adam is not his son, and he longed to have a little boy. After he split with Caroline, the Aldridges decided to have another baby to cement their marriage. But when Alice arrived, and he was told she was a girl, he walked out of the hospital and went to the races with Mandy Beesborough. If it had been a boy he'd have stayed, I'm sure.

Brian is exactly the same age as me, we went to the same school, and many of his family circumstances have run parallel with my own life. Brian brought up Adam and Debbie, just as I did with Toby and Barney, and like the Aldridges, we have a daughter of our own. I would like to say, however, that I don't feel the same way about Jane as Brian felt about Alice and I was delighted when our little girl was born. Nor do I share his wandering eye.

And – can you credit it? – my first wife was called Jennifer and Judy's first husband was called Brian. And I ended up in Britain's longest-running soap opera, playing a character called Brian who is married to Jennifer. Extraordinary.

In 1987, a year or so after the Caroline fling, *The Archers* won a Sony Gold award and, very kindly, the BBC thought they'd give us a posh lunch at Broadcasting House to celebrate. Come the day, we had a huge phalanx of actors outside the BBC for photographs and then everyone went up to the lunch. Judy wasn't feeling well that day so she just sat nursing a glass of mineral water, and didn't touch the food, mercifully.

Like any actor offered free food, I gobbled the lot, so I scoffed platefuls of cold meat and salad and thought no more about it. Exactly a month later, on a Monday morning, I was due to go to Birmingham to record *The Archers*. Usually, we would go to work however ill we may feel – as I mentioned, we've had people taken in wheelchairs, almost on stretchers, to record – but on this particular morning I simply couldn't get out of bed. I felt dreadful. Judy was also recording on that day, so she phoned the studio on my behalf, left the bedroom curtains drawn and went up to Birmingham. A few hours later she rang. 'If it's any consolation,' she said, 'they're dropping like flies up here.'

Four of the actors, as well as the assistant producer and the then editor, Liz Rigbey, had come down with hepatitis A. Thankfully, Judy had been on the Perrier and stayed away from the cold meat. We learned later that there had been somebody in the kitchens at Broadcasting House who was a hepatitis carrier and hadn't washed his hands, so had passed it on through the food. We were suddenly very ill, very yellow and we couldn't work for over two months. It was a horrible illness.

For three months I ate nothing but fruit, lost an enormous amount of weight and was bright yellow, including the palms of my hands. Friends would come to see me and wish me well, then I would watch them whispering to each other as they walked away, and I'd think, 'Blimey, they don't think they're going to see me again.'

Although still ill, and feeling as weak as a kitten, when I returned to work it was to begin my flirtation with Betty Tucker. Believe me, it is not easy being sexy on air when you're bright yellow and barely able to get out of a chair. Now that's what I call acting!

It took a year to recover, a year of no alcohol and abstinence from almost everything actually – and when I say everything I mean *everything*! I made a full recovery but my liver has never gone back to the way it was before. I get a hangover more quickly, I get liverish more than I used to, but that's possibly a good thing, because it means I'm a bit more moderate in my intake.

Throughout my illness, Judy was still working but at least she was spared the chore of cooking for me, because I was living on fruit and water. It was a cheap year.

Exactly twelve months after that lunch I was given the all-clear to have a drink, so Judy went out and bought the most stonkingly expensive bottle of red wine, far more than we'd ever spent before, and cooked a delicious meal to go with it. After one glass I was slurring and after two I fell asleep. 'I hope we're not going to have this forever,' Judy thought. 'Or the next fifty years could be fairly boring.' Fortunately, my tolerance level recovered very quickly and it takes a little more than one glass to make me fall asleep now.

ELEVEN

The Comedians

Throughout my career I have had the thrill of working with many comedians, but perhaps the oddest pairing was my stint with Bernard Manning on his 1981 quiz show, *Under Manning*. Each programme featured eccentric members of the public who would do crazy things such as sleep in their beds with snakes, or throw custard pies at each other and pretend they were clowns. Bernard would interview them and insult them and would banter with me. I was supposed to be the antithesis of Bernard, which I found fairly flattering. There I was, dressed head to toe in bespoke tailoring, looking rather distinguished, like a young Nicholas Parsons, and I would ask the quiz questions.

There were, apparently, thousands of applications for the job and, to my amazement when they'd whittled it down to the last six, I was one of them. We were taken up to Bernard's spiritual home, The Embassy Club in Manchester, on a Saturday evening and, in front of his adoring fans, we went on stage with him, one after the other, as the producer and director watched from the front to make their final choice. It was me!

The producer was Jeremy Fox, and at dinner one evening I asked him whom he would have chosen for the show if he hadn't had Bernard. 'Les Dawson,' was his reply. Now, if it had been Les Dawson I think the show would have run for years, but I didn't realize then that the media as a whole didn't approve of Bernard Manning and, looking back now, I could understand why, although I wouldn't say a word against him because working together we got along famously.

I once asked Bernard which comics made him laugh, and he said, 'You're funnier than most.' Typical! But I think I made him laugh because he'd never ever met anybody like me. He thought I was 'fraitfully' upper class – 'Posher than Prince Charles', he used to say.

'Do you know Charles,' he once told me, 'when I go home at the end of the week, my wife says, "You've been with that Charles, haven't you? You're talking a bit posh."'

'That's funny, Bernard,' I replied. 'Because when I go home to my wife she says just the opposite!'

Backstage, between shows, Bernard loved to walk around in nothing but his underpants and on one occasion, he appeared at my dressing room door, this white flabby body with his pants pulled up just under his nipples. I turned round and said, 'Did I give you permission to hang your stomach in my dressing room?' He fell about – well, wobbled about actually.

History puts Bernard down as a racist. I put him down as a poorly educated man from a certain group of society, who never intended to be racist. I've met a lot more dangerous and more insidiously racist people in this world than Bernard Manning. And, as a comic, in his day, he was one of the best.

To my great surprise, ten years after *Under Manning*, the producer Bryan Izzard, whom I'd never hit it off with on Bernard's show, asked me to take part in an episode of *Tonight at 8.30*, the BBC production of Noël Coward's one-act plays. The cast included Joan Collins, John Alderton and the late Denis Quilley, who subsequently became a dear friend.

I had always lusted after Joan Collins. When I was younger I thought she was gorgeous, just the most beautiful creature. Way back when I was teaching I even had a girlfriend who looked

ABOVE: My parents' final home, Carter's Meadow, Charlton, Hants. Precious last years together.

BELOW: Edgar Harrison (Dan Archer) celebrates his Golden Wedding, with (left to right) Mollie Harris (Martha Woodford), Norman Painting (Phil Archer), Patricia Greene (Jill Archer), Bob Arnold (Tom Forrest), Edgar and his wife Kay, myself, Judy Bennett (Shula Archer), Graham Roberts (George Barford), June Spencer (Peggy Archer) and Hilary Newcombe (Polly Perks). *(Cedric Barker)*

ABOVE: Rehearsing for an *Archers* show in Liverpool. Left to right: George Barford (Graham Roberts), Neil Carter (Brian Hewlett), Eddie Grundy (Trevor Harrison), Brian (C.C.), Tom Forrest (Bob Arnold), Shula Archer (Judy Bennett) and Phil Archer (Norman Painting) at the piano. *(© BBC)*

RIGHT: The eccentric scorer on *Noel's House Party*. *(© BBC)*

LEFT: With Bernard Manning at the Embassy Club, singing 'By the Light of the Silvery Moon'.

ABOVE: Judy standing with Nigel Miles-Thomas and Natalie Bohm, while I sit with our stage manager Born Yuen, after rehearsing *Relatively Speaking* in Singapore, 1996.

RIGHT: What a treat! The Queen's Garden Party 1998, and the heat was tremendous. My hat stuck to my head and Judy's heel blistered – but it was well worth it!

LEFT: I was honoured to be part of a small invited group of performers to meet Her Majesty the Queen. In the background, David Jacobs and Nicholas Parsons.
(© BBC)

LEFT: The fiftieth anniversary of *The Archers*. Prince Charles kindly hosted a party for us at St James's Palace. *(Paul Burns)*

RIGHT: A welcome cone in Osterley Park during an *Archers* event for the public. Don't ask why I'm wearing my school 1st XI blazer, I've no idea. Rather impressed it still fitted though!

BELOW: My only appearance in the middle at Lords. A proud day but stumped for 18! Front row, centre, Clive Radley (Middlesex and England), front row left, Harry Latchman (Middlesex).

ABOVE: What a surprise! My reward for being the nation's most notorious philanderer. What a night, Judy and I got to bed at 5 a.m., and me with my new hip as well! 29 January 2003. (*Freemantle Media*)

ABOVE: The Count and Countess Actursocsoff. Judy and I as guests of dear friends Richard and Jackie Caring at the charity fancy dress ball in aid of the Children's Charity, Catherine's Palace, St Petersburg. Simply the best party of our lives.

ABOVE: Barney, Jane and Toby, all grown up. When little, they called me 'Baldilocks and the three hairs'; when they grew up they called me 'Spamhead'!

RIGHT: Jane, my lovely daughter, as she is today. (*George Ktistakis*)

LEFT: Mick Brownfield's amazing drawing for the *Radio Times* when Brian and Siobhan were at the heights of passion ... It's not really like that on radio, damn it!

BELOW: In the studio with the Tuckers, Mike (Terry Molloy) and Betty (Pam Craig). Sadly, Betty was killed off when Pam emigrated to New Zealand a few years ago! *(© BBC)*

ABOVE: Ashore in a Greek taverna – what fun we had. Left to right: Me, Tim Rice, Andrew Dean (Hoss), Richard Stilgoe, Peter Skellern, Martin Young and Alex Armitage.

BELOW: Trafalgar Night, 2006. Dinner onboard *HMS Victory*, as guests of Second Sea Lord Adrian Johns. Sometimes the name Collingwood comes in handy! *(© Crown Copyright)*

ABOVE: Introducing to fellow guests Tim Bentinck (David Archer) and Tamsin Grieg (Debbie Aldridge) at our joint 65th birthday treat at Annabel's in 2008. Thanks a million, Richard and Jackie.

ABOVE RIGHT: The Reverend Collingwood conducting a funeral service in the TV sitcom *Bob Martin*.

RIGHT: 'The sexiest bastard in show business'. Taken at King Edward VII Hospital, London, the day after my hip replacement operation, by my 'dear friend' Richard Stilgoe!

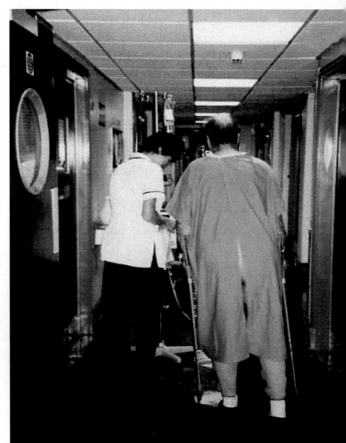

like Joan Collins, and how grateful I was! On the day of the read-through, I sat down next to Joan, searching for tucks. Nothing! Just beautiful bone structure and a lovely face.

Joan was such fun to work with. We were rehearsing in the BBC Acton rehearsal rooms and, at coffee breaks, we ordinary mortals drank our coffee out of polystyrene cups, but not Joanie. She brought her own bone china cup and saucer! Such style – what a star!

Even so, she was a company girl and enjoyed a laugh on set. During the technical rehearsal, I was standing beside Joan and she was wearing the most wonderful pair of designer jeans, a leather belt, a white blouse, no make-up, hair pulled back with a band, and she still looked wonderful.

'Joan, you are marvellous, darling.' I blurted. 'How do you keep such a fantastic figure?'

To my joy, she fell to the floor and proceeded to do press-ups, and as she did them she looked up at me over her shoulder and said, 'This is how I keep my figure, Charles.'

And at that moment some twerp tapped me on the shoulder and said, 'Excuse me, Charles, can I talk about your Equity subscription?'

'Piss off!' I said. 'Can't you see? Joan Collins is doing press-ups for me! Who cares about my bloody subs?'

The recording over, we went to the bar, where Joan was having a large gin, and bought me one too.

'It's been so lovely meeting you,' I said as we left.

She gave me a kiss and said, 'We must meet for lunch sometime.'

I thought, 'Oh, yes please!' and I went home and told Judy. If my memory serves me right, Judy was in full make-up and high heels for breakfast for the following fortnight.

Through Richard Stilgoe, I met a true 'man of show business', Mike Craig. He was *the* authority on variety theatre, having written numerous books on the subject, and was Head of Comedy in Manchester, where much of the radio comedy was produced. In those days, on Radio 4 and Radio 2, many of the well-known comics like Harry Worth and Jack Smethurst had their own half-hour shows and, while recording *Stilgoe's Around*, Mike and I hit it off.

When a new series of Roy Castle's programme, *Castle's Corner*, was coming up, Mike kindly suggested me to one of his writing partners, Ron McDonald, who was also a comedy producer at Manchester. Ron took me on as Roy Castle's sidekick for three years, making batches of twelve shows each year. We recorded the show, in front of an audience, at the Paris Theatre in Regent Street and at Watford Palace.

Roy was the nicest man I've ever worked with. And when I say Roy was the nicest person I ever worked with, he was even nicer than that. He knew I'd worked with Bernard Manning, and he recalled the time he was booked to work with Bernard for a 'charity do' at the Grosvenor House Hotel in London.

'I can't work with Bernard, not with my act,' Roy told his agent. 'I'm a serious Christian, a clean guy, trumpet, dance and television. I can't do it with Bernard.'

'Don't worry, Roy,' his agent assured him. 'You're on *before* Bernard. Bernard follows *you*.'

So he agreed to the gig.

'I turned up at Grosvenor House at 9.30, to go at ten o'clock and, to my horror, Bernard was already on,' Roy told me. 'There was nothing I could do. So I stood in the wings, Bernard came off and on I went. I always began with the trumpet, so I walked on, started to play the trumpet and two thousand people got up and danced!

Roy was full of silly stories. He told me that once, when doing his cabaret act at the Savoy Hotel, the announcement came over the Tannoy, 'Now, Ladies and Gentleman, the star of the show, Mr Roy Castle!' His opening number was 'One, two, Button Your Shoe', and he thought he'd had a wonderful idea for his entrance. He stood in the wings and tapped the microphone with his finger so the audience heard it, and as he tapped he said, 'One, two, *(tap)* one two, *(tap)* one, two *(tap)*... one, two, button your shoe, put on your coat and hat ...' and then he walked on stage singing the song. At the end of the number, a voice from the audience shouted, 'Couldn't you have practised all that this afternoon?'

One of my treasured memories of *Castle's Corner* was the guest appearance of Eric Morecambe at the Watford Palace in 1984, just two weeks before he died. When Eric turned up in the early afternoon to rehearse, he looked wonderful: he was immaculately dressed in a three-piece suit and he announced his arrival with a 'Heh heh heh heh' from the wings as his trilby hat flew like a Frisbee across the stage. In rehearsal, Eric was absolutely on the button, sticking to the script word for word.

'Eric,' said Roy. 'During the show I'm going to sing "Tiger Rag", and I want you to play the trombone. When I sing "Hold that tiger", I want you to give me a sliding blast on the trombone.'

Of course, Eric didn't have a clue how to play the trombone, but as long as he could get some noise out of it, it would be funny. That night, as we recorded, Roy introduced, 'My oldest friend, the one and only Eric Morecambe,' and Watford Palace rocked. Eric came on to tumultuous applause and we started the sketch but, out of the corner of his eye, Roy was horrified to see Eric fold up the script and put it in his pocket. He had decided he could be a lot funnier ad-libbing than anything he had read in rehearsals.

Somewhere I have a tape of the show where you can clearly hear Roy rather plaintively saying, 'Eric, script! What about your script?' Eric busked it all and, of course, it was sensational. The two of them, despite the odd interjection from me, were just hilarious. When the sketch was over, after Roy had sung 'Tiger Rag' with Eric's assistance on trombone, he was supposed to put the trombone down centre stage, by the microphone, and leave it there. Not Eric. He took it into the wings. Roy and I carried on doing the remainder of the show but, every time there was the slightest pause, Eric would give yet another blast of trombone from the wings.

Performance over, I went home and woke Judy, to tell her, 'Darling I've just worked with Eric Morecambe, what a night I've had!'

'What was he like?' she asked, knowing his history of heart attacks.

'He seemed fine and he looked wonderful,' I said. 'But he's quite small and delicate looking, like a china ornament.' Two weeks later he died, having just left the stage at the Roses Theatre in Tewkesbury, where he had performed with Stan Stennett. This delicate ornament shattered and the nation lost a legend, but I had my golden day with Eric. Lucky me!

Another great comic I shared airtime with was Harry Worth. I did two or three series with him at Leeds City Varieties, a beautiful theatre, where they used to record *The Good Old Days*. Despite his bumbling persona, Harry was in fact very bright and, as luck would have it, he happened to be an *Archers* fan too. Off air, he was just like his performance suggested: he delivered a line with expert timing, but sometimes he got a bit muddled. At the end of each programme Mike Craig, who was directing, went through the retakes and, on one occasion, he said, 'Harry, we'll just do the last page of that scene again, because you're getting the stress wrong on that line.'

So we did it again, and he got it wrong again. Mike suggested another way, and he got it wrong again. I could sense that Harry didn't quite get it, so I made a joke of it in front of the audience.

'Harry, may I have a word?'

'My dear boy, of course.'

'Michael, will you give us a moment?' Mike was in the outside broadcast van listening to us, the audience were rocking with laughter, so I took Harry by the arm and I said, 'What he means is – this,' and I showed him.

'Ohhh!' said Harry. This time he got it dead right. He looked at the audience, then at me, and, with his infectious laugh, said, 'I hate him. He's always right.' It was just lovely.

I truly admired all the comics I have worked with. In another world I would love to have been a stand-up comedian myself. The closest I get is my one-man show, which I enjoy. There's nothing more satisfying than trying to entertain people on your own – as long as you can pull it off.

In 1989, I was asked to do an episode of *Hannay* and in my first scene I was to meet Robert Powell, as the title character, off the train at King's Cross Station in London. Very early that morning, I was in the make-up van near the station, it was a nice May day, the sun was out and, sitting next to me, was Sharon Maugham, Robert's co-star in the series. In came the director, Henry Herbert, who was a sort of bouncy, tall, eccentric-looking chap in gym shoes. Sharon knew him of old, so she greeted him with, 'Hello Henry, how are you? Did you come up this morning, or did you stay in London?'

'I stayed in London,' he answered, then turned to me and said, 'Hello, Charles, I'm the director, Henry Herbert.'

'Lovely to meet you,' I said. 'Whereabouts in the country do you live?'

'Salisbury.'

'Oh, how lovely,' I said. 'That's great. I was brought up round there. And I went to school in Dorset.'

He told me he had a son who would soon be going to school.

'Are you thinking of sending him to Sherborne?' I asked.

'I might have a look,' he said.

'Do,' I went on. 'But school fees are so expensive now and the price of property in Salisbury is not cheap, so finding the money can be tough, these days.'

'Oh yes, of course it is,' he replied. 'I don't know how we'll manage it.'

As we chatted, I noticed that Sharon seemed to be wiping tears from her eyes quite a lot, and I thought, 'I do hope she's all right.'

It was only after Henry left that the floodgates opened and I discovered she was crying with laughter.

'What are you laughing at?' I asked.

'You do know who he is, don't you?' she screeched.

'Yes, he's Henry Herbert. He's the director.'

'Yes, he is,' she told me. 'But there you are telling him the price of property in Salisbury's expensive and the school fees are terrible – he is Henry Herbert, that's his name as a director, but actually he's the Earl of Pembroke, and he owns Wilton House. You sounded like you thought he lived in a little semi in the suburbs of Salisbury!'

It was wicked and very funny that Henry Herbert didn't tell me that at the time. He just let me bury myself and, typically, I kept digging!

TWELVE

Brian Lives!

As we were living in North London, Toby and Barney attended Highgate School and, in the early eighties, Judy and I saw a school production of the *Roses of Eyam*, a drama about the plague. Lloyd Owen, who went on to star in the West End and became famous in *Monarch of the Glen*, played the lead, opposite a striking dark-haired girl from Camden School for Girls. At the end of the performance, Judy and I agreed that the two leads were quite sensational. They just had something more than most school-age actors.

A few years later, in 1991, I was at Pebble Mill and *The Archers'* editor Vanessa Whitburn told me, 'As you know we've cast the part of Debbie, your stepdaughter. We've given it to a young actress called Tamsin Greig, and she's coming in today to record her first episode. Perhaps you'd go and meet her at reception, take her for lunch and just show her the ropes?'

I was only too pleased, so I met her and we went up to the canteen for some lunch. While we were chatting, I interrupted her and said, 'I've seen you before, I know it.' She looked puzzled and I continued, 'Did you go to Camden School, and did you play the lead in *Roses of Eyam* at Highgate School?'

'Yes,' she replied.

'You were absolutely brilliant,' I said. From that day on, working with Tamsin has always had a sort of special added quality for me. In fact, over the years we have enjoyed working together so much that there was a time when people almost used to wonder if it was slightly incestuous, whether Brian rather fancied Debbie. It isn't like that at all, but we do get on extremely well. It was no surprise when Tamsin's great talent was recognized in both comedy and drama.

To my great joy, Tamsin still values the part of Debbie and continues to play her whenever she's available. She hasn't as much time as she once had, so very cleverly Vanessa, not wanting to lose Tamsin, had Brian buy into a consortium that bought an estate in Hungary, and then sent Debbie out to manage it, which is ideal. So, in between her great television projects and plays, when Tamsin has a few weeks off, surprise, surprise, Debbie flies over and has farming chats with Brian. She gives him a few lectures on behaving himself too, commiserates with her mother, has a row with her brother, tickles her little sister, goes and sees her granny and then she's off to Hungary again with her mother's plea of 'Do stay longer next time,' ringing in her ears. It works really well for everybody.

As well as having an award-winning career in television, Tamsin has lovely children and we are very close as families. Finally, her talented husband is actor and writer Rick Leaf, so her married name is Mrs T Leaf. Love it!

Tamsin isn't the only young actress who has become a TV star while working on *The Archers*. Lucy Davis played Hayley Jordan for ten years from 1995 and had to undergo a kidney transplant during that time. She came into the programme, a young bubbly, instinctive, comic actress and everybody loved the character of Hayley. Then all of a sudden, Lucy was playing the secretary in Ricky Gervais's comedy *The Office* and she now lives and works in LA, where she's doing incredibly well, with her handsome husband, actor Owain Yeoman.

Judy and I were thrilled to be invited to their wedding, in

December 2006. And what an event that was! It was held in the crypt chapel in St Paul's Cathedral, which was only allowed because her father, Jasper Carrot, was awarded an OBE four years earlier.

I've been very fortunate with the casting of my soap family. As well as Tamsin and Angie, we have June Spencer as Brian's mother-in-law, Peggy. June is one of the original cast and, as I write, is about to celebrate her ninetieth birthday. She is a phenomenal actress and has always slightly scared me. That may be down to the fact that, when I first joined the cast, I used to stay at the Holiday Inn and use their swimming pool. June also stayed there and, with her hourglass figure and perfect hair, would swim up and down while I swam as far away as possible, trying not to splash her. To me, she is a star. She was one of those people for whom you stood to attention, and I still rather do. I admire her enormously. How many other people of ninety do you know who work at all, let alone being capable of giving such a stunning performance as she has?

During the harrowing storyline of Jack's Alzheimer's in the winter of 2008, the BBC gave us a Christmas party and June came along. She looked marvellous. She wore a little black cocktail number, pretty jewels and high-heeled shoes. The look in her eyes said, 'I'm the star of the show at the moment, I've got the big storyline,' and she thoroughly enjoyed herself.

The following morning I asked her how she was and June said, 'I've got a bit of a headache this morning because I drank rather a lot of red wine last night.'

Fantastic! I want to be on whatever she's on.

The other members of the family are Kellie Bright as Kate, Holly Chapman as Alice and Andrew Wincott as Adam. When a new character is to be cast, one of the current cast members reads in at the audition, so I was present when Adam was chosen. Eighteen different actors were short-listed and we auditioned them all in one day. I thought Andrew was very impressive and I'm glad he got the part. He's a fine actor.

Kellie Bright was a child actress who starred as Joe McGann's daughter in *The Upper Hand,* and coincidentally, I played her uncle in one episode long before she was my daughter Kate in *The Archers.* She has done a lot of TV and film, including *Ali G Indahouse* where she was the legendary 'Me Julie', and the recent *Horne and Corden* series. Her character lives in South Africa at present so she isn't around that often, but when she's there, she's pure gold.

But the most recent, wonderful surprise has been little Holly Chapman who plays Brian's youngest, Alice. She was at Sylvia Young's stage school and came in to the show aged twelve. She's an instinctive actress and as each year passes she gets better and better. Angie and I, in a sort of parental way, feel we're blessed to have such strong actors playing members of the family.

Among the young actors, most of whom I won't mention for fear of leaving somebody out, we also have the very successful Felicity Jones who plays Emma Carter. Like Tamsin, her career has really taken off, with roles in the film versions of *The Tempest* and *Brideshead Revisited* as well as numerous TV appearances. As I write she is about to make Ricky Gervais's comedy film *Cemetery Junction*, so she is big news.

We haven't always been so lucky in the casting. We had one young lad who came in to play one of Kate's many boyfriends. I hadn't actually had any scenes with him up to this point, and one day I arrived in the greenroom to find everybody was fuming so I asked what was wrong.

'That conceited young guy,' one of the others said. 'He simply goes in the studio and lays the pages of his script out on the table, and takes up the whole space. He pays no attention to anybody else in the scene, where they want to stand or anything. He's so arrogant!'

'Leave him to me,' I said. 'I'm in the next episode with him.'

He was very charming when I met him in the greenroom but hugely above himself, considering he was just starting out. Come the next episode, we went in and there he was. I stood and watched him as he laid out page one, page two, three and four right across the table, with no thought for any of us. I calmly gathered his papers up from the table, tidied them into a pile, handed them back to him and said, 'Young man, there is a pecking order around here, and you're at the bottom of it!'

All the young actors at the moment are very strong, and gradually they will replace us, which is as it should be. Thinking back to when I joined *The Archers* I hope I'm not like some of the older cast members who resented me. You could see them thinking, 'Are these young bucks going to replace us?' We probably were, but that's the way of the world. The thing about *The Archers*, and one of the reasons I believe it has lasted so long, is that it has a timescale and a generational gap of its own, just like real life. Actors have started as young characters, grown older in the show and have now died, with the next generation coming up behind them. It's hard to accept but I'm now one of the older ones and personally I would like to carry on until *I* fall over, not Brian. Brian will die, I hope, when I do. I think that is part of the magic: the listener gets thoroughly involved with the characters and, to a much lesser extent, with the actors who play them.

As I mentioned, when I began my lifelong stint as Brian Aldridge, Dan and Doris were very much the King and Queen of the show. *The Archers* is, after all, the title of the programme and it's very important that the Archers as a family should feature in the public's mind as the backbone of the village.

We're very fortunate that the actors who play members of the Archer family today are still loved by all. Timothy Bentinck, who plays David Archer, is another one of those actors who's able to bring a lot more to the part. Essentially, David is not a particularly exciting character, he's a run-of-the-mill country farmer, but in every scene that Timothy plays, he brings such realism and we're lucky that he's the one who's playing the part and carrying the family flag.

However, pride of place on *The Archers* throne must really go to Patricia Greene, who plays Jill. Paddy has been a backbone of the programme for over fifty years – after signing a six-week contract in 1957! And she has brought a warmth to her performance that no other character in the programme has, mainly because she is such a warm person herself. As Paddy, she has a wicked sense of humour and she has a wonderful cackling laugh that you can hear a mile away, but underneath it all beats the heart of one of the kindest people I've ever known. She was a fine stage actress who has, because of the way things panned out, devoted most of her life to playing Jill. Judy and I both love her dearly.

Graham Blockey, who plays Lynda Snell's long-suffering husband Robert, leads a double life. When he's not playing Robert Snell he's a GP in Farnham, which is tough on him because, with a cast full of hypochondriacs, the minute he walks in the greenroom we all line up at surgery, saying, 'Could you have a look at this? Could you listen to this?'

I couldn't write about about *The Archers* without mentioning the Grundys. The Grundys were always there really, but when they got the opportunity to be high profile, Trevor Harrison, in particular, took the bull by the horns and turned Eddie into a cult figure. Over the years, through all the ups and downs, Trevor has never changed, and never let his success go to his head. He's a valued friend and some time ago was awarded an MBE. Thoroughly deserved – just as long as I get a knighthood!

Eddie's wife Clarrie has been played by three different actresses. The first Clarrie, Heather Bell, stormed out after a row with William Smethurst; the second, Fiona Mathieson, tragically took her own life in 1987; and the part is now played by Rosalind Adams, one of the many established radio perfomers to come into *The Archers* alongside such talents as Judy, Patricia Gallimore who plays Pat and Edward Kelsey, who is Joe. Terry Molloy, who plays Mike Tucker, Brian Hewlett (Neil Carter) and Carole Boyd (Lynda Snell) were also established broadcast actors before joining the show, as were many more, and every one of them brings something more to the part than the creators of the characters could possibly have thought of in the first place.

Colin Skipp has played Tony Archer for forty years and is very talented. Colin and I were at RADA together and, back then, he was always so serious. I don't think he approved of my light-hearted approach to life.

The character of Oliver Sterling is played by Michael Cochrane, again a radio regular as well as performing on stage and television. He brings a great quality to everything he does, and is wickedly funny off air. 'Cocky' as he's known to all also sounds rather like me, so every now and again the audience get a bit confused between Oliver and Brian and, in fact, at one read-through we decided to swap roles for a short while, so I read a bit of his scene and he read a bit of mine, and nobody noticed!

People often ask me whether the cast is like a big family and I would say it has its similarities, in that we get on well most of the time, if not *all* the time. As with any workplace, there are certain people that when you walk in the greenroom you just sit there and make polite conversation. On another day you can walk in and be thrilled at who is there, but that's the way of the world.

We only meet up for a period of six days once a month, so by and large we can't wait to catch up on news, any scandal and what else we've been up to. It's all fairly trivial, but it's green-room chat with a lot of 'Darling, you were so good in so-and-so' and 'Oh, you'll be marvellous in that!' The majority of the actors have done an awful lot more than just being in *The Archers*, more than perhaps the public realize.

One thing that always impresses new cast members is the speed with which we record the programme. We only get two-and-a-quarter hours to record an episode, which normally involves six or seven scenes, and then there's all the technical work that has to take place to get it ready for broadcast.

The technique for radio is very different from TV and theatre. One actor, sadly no longer with us, came in to play the vicar a while back and his performance was enormous. It was too theatrical, too colourful, too extravagant. The late, great Margot Boyd, who played Mrs Antrobus, took him on one side.

'Darling,' she said. 'You're doing too much.'

'What do you mean?' he asked, rather affronted. 'I'm an actor, darling!'

'I know you are,' she assured him. 'You're a very good actor, but this is *The Archers*, and you're doing too much. Watch those who have been in it for a long time. They do practically nothing; just a little more than perhaps you might at home, to make it interesting. Their energy level is a little higher than in real life, but they're doing nothing, just watch them.'

Unfortunately he didn't watch us, and his character didn't last very long.

People occasionally ask, 'Do you really act on radio?' It's a fair question, I suppose, but *of course* we do. It's quite like acting on television, and to a lesser extent on stage; the only difference is that we have the scripts in our hands because we don't learn it and we don't require costume and make-up.

The most important thing to learn is what's called 'microphone technique'. We have to be constantly aware of the microphone. You can't turn away from it or the audience won't hear you. For example, if I'm leaving a room or walking away from Adam in the field and you hear me calling back, 'I'll see you later in the pub. Keep up the good work,' I don't turn away from him. I have to back away so that my head is still physically facing the microphone. No surprise, then, that those who join us with no radio experience can get very confused.

Radio fans are always riveted when they come to visit *The Archers'* studio, which is now at The Mail Box in the centre of Birmingham. We moved there, in 2004, after thirty-three years at the Pebble Mill studios, but the layout of the set remains remarkably similar.

The studio comprises four acting areas. We have a large, empty echoing area, which is used for airport lounges, large barns or village hall events, and then a smaller, cosier section, with sofas, curtains and carpet, where we play the sitting room scenes, the lounge bar scenes and, as far I'm concerned, the bedroom scenes with Siobhan. Tragically, a few years later, this is also where Caroline Lennon lay on a sofa recording Siobhan's dying scenes.

Moving through a door, which is not a solid door but a piece of scenery on wheels, we find the kitchen area, which is used for all the kitchens in the village. There is an actual cooker, a fridge, a table and a washbasin with taps. I'd like to point out that it also has an Aga, which we at Home Farm use – Angie Piper wouldn't settle for anything less! – whereas the ordinary mortals just have a bog standard cooker.

The kitchen 'set' is also used as the public bar in The Bull, where the drinks are served and where over the years, I have drunk pints and pints of water, never beer or tea – sadly!

The whole studio is a huge rectangle, so the areas are set out quite easily. We walk from the kitchen area into 'the dead room' – so named because the walls are lined with polystyrene foam to prevent atmospheric noise, so when we speak there is no echo and no reverberation. There, we record all the external scenes, because the sound engineers are then able to overlay all the birdsong, the tractors, or the gunshot or whatever is required, as we are recording.

There are also a lot of props and, while I wouldn't want to give away too much, suffice it to say that when it's lambing time at Home Farm there's a lot of expended audiotape, a wet towel and a tub of yoghurt! Fortunately it's not me who has to get into a mess, but the spot effects person, who gets on his knees with handfuls of yoghurt, pretending that he is shoving his hand up the nether regions of a sheep, while I'm grunting, 'Come on, shove!' They play in a lot of sheep effect noises and finish with a tiny bleat at the end for the newborn lamb, as a wet towel is dropped onto the pile of tape, and the nation thinks another lamb's been born. Marvellous.

When Brian and Jennifer are having a refreshing gin and tonic by the Home Farm pool and you hear the clinking of ice on the side of the glass, you needn't be jealous. Again, it's only water and the ice cubes are actually a couple of dominoes.

The last little secret I will share with you is the sound of the five-bar gate. I can't count the number of times I've released the sheep from one pen to another with Adam. Each time one of our excellent spot effects boys or girls is standing there with a very old metal ironing board, and the clunk of the legs of the ironing board against the top of it makes exactly the right sound. I believe if somebody ever shouted 'Fire!' the one thing that we'd want to save would be that old ironing board! We couldn't live without it.

Considering we are recording twenty-four episodes in a week, the writing is consistently of a high standard. On the whole, I think the writing has improved since I first joined and some of the storylines that the Aldridges have had have been thought through brilliantly.

In 1989, Brian fell victim to the BSE outbreak in the most bizarre way. He was knocked over by one of Eddie Grundy's BSE-ridden cows, smashed his head on the cowshed floor and consequently suffered post-traumatic epilepsy.

Brian had been having a run of bad luck as it was, but this time he ended up in hospital on a life support machine and no sooner had he got over that than he got the epilepsy shock. I, for one, began to get very concerned for Brian's future. With every script I opened I feared the worst: that the BBC were going to kill him off. I could see the foreign holidays and new car going straight out the window.

The editor at the time was Ruth Patterson and one day, on my way to the studio, she stopped me and said, 'Charles, can I have a word?' Gulp! 'Oh Lord, here it comes,' I thought.

'Yes, Ruth, what is it?' I replied, as calmly as possible.

'I've noticed how anxious you've become recently, so I wanted to give you something.' And out of a brown package she pulled a white T-shirt, which she'd had specially printed with the words, 'Brian Lives!' Bless her.

In 1991 our current editor, Vanessa Whitburn, arrived, and she wasted no time in giving Brian some fantastic storylines. Jennifer went and had an affair with her previous husband, Roger Travers-Macy, hotly followed by Kate going missing, presumed dead. Credit where credit's due, Vanessa cleverly made sure that the writers kept the timescale realistic. Kate disappeared in autumn and didn't turn up again until the following Easter, so, as in life, Brian and Jennifer and all at Home Farm had to endure birthdays and Christmas, New Year's Eve, all the while not knowing whether Kate was alive or dead.

Not surprisingly, it all got too much for Brian and, while pouring his heart out to Phil Archer's sympathetic ear, he broke down and cried his eyes out.

As I read the script for that episode on the train from London to Birmingham, I reeled with horror when I read the stage directions, 'Brian breaks down and cries.' I had never been required to cry before, either on TV or radio, and I didn't know if I'd be able to manage it. I carefully reread the scene when Brian is explaining to Phil that he doesn't have any idea where Kate is or whether she is even alive and I decided, each time I read it, to substitute the name of my daughter Jane instead of Kate.

So there I was, sitting on the train, imagining what it would be like if Jane went missing in the same way and, before I knew it, tears were streaming down my face, prompting concern from the man sitting opposite me.

When I got to the studio, I was confident I could reproduce the same emotions. And as I played the scene with Norman Painting, tears were really streaming down my face again. Of course, to the listener I was Brian talking about Kate, but inside I was thinking about Jane.

With so many characters, it's inevitable that none of us are universally liked. All of the major characters have their supporters, who write to us or send emails saying, 'You're my favourite', but for every positive comment there's somebody else who writes, 'I can't stand you, you drive me mad', and that's fair game. I don't think it matters; you just don't want the audience not to care either way.

Judy and I were at a garden centre recently, and we were

looking at a display and I saw a packet of seeds I wanted, picked them up, turned round and said, 'These would be good, wouldn't they, darling?' And the lady standing behind me wasn't Judy but a total stranger. She smiled and replied, 'You can call me darling any time you like, Brian.'

When fans approach us it's nearly always very light-hearted, I don't think anybody's ever been really horrid to me. However, I was once introduced to a man at Lord's cricket ground, who was the headmaster of a prep school, and my friend said, 'This is Charles Collingwood, he plays Brian in *The Archers*.'

He shook my hand and said, 'I'm sorry but I've never listened to your little programme.'

'That's all right,' I retorted. 'I've never heard of your little school.'

He was furious, but he hadn't realized how rude he'd been himself.

THIRTEEN

A Russian Soap

'Do you fancy three days in Moscow, darling?' A question my agent Hilary put to me in early December 1992.

'Why?' I asked, suspiciously.

'It seems they are starting a radio soap along the lines of *The Archers* and they want one of the cast to go and talk to the actors.'

Liz Rigbey, our much-loved former editor, had been in Moscow for over a year setting up this most enterprising venture – a daily Russian soap called *Dom Syem, Podjezd Chetirie* which translates as *House Seven, Entrance Four*. Well, what's in a title?

Of course, I agreed.

A few days later, on the 17 December, I found myself in a taxi heading for Heathrow airport, to catch the 9.50 morning flight to Moscow. Assorted leather-clad Russians checked in before me, plus one fat, eccentric Brit, bald, with huge sideburns, smelly clothes and a mass of assorted luggage. I was relieved to hear he was going to France.

At passport control, I got a pleasant surprise when the gruff-looking man poring over my passport said, 'You're Brian, aren't you?' It gave me rather a glow, knowing that all was not lost! On the plane, however, it transpired that none of the crew were *Archers'* fans, which left me a bit deflated until the pilot, who was, invited me to the flight deck. It's always fascinating and somewhat reassuring to meet the pilot and co-pilot so, after a couple of photos and two Ambridge pens for their trouble, I returned to my seat for a nice lunch and a small bottle of Fleurie, which was unfortunately ice cold. When I popped it between my legs to warm it up I got some strange looks from the chap opposite, so I put it under my arm instead.

At Moscow Airport, which looks pretty much like any other, I had been warned that the passport checks and luggage retrieval could take up to two hours but, apart from a hairy moment when a humourless Russian demanded to examine my radio, it all went swimmingly and I was through in half an hour. I waited and waited as endless men in fur hats shouted 'Taxi!' and finally I spotted a pretty young girl with a large piece of paper bearing my name in green capital letters.

'Hello, sorry I'm late,' she said. 'I'm Vicki. You were so quick you beat me to it.'

With my new Russian friend, I slid through the slush as she assured me, 'Today has been like spring'. It was cold, but not too cold and the car, which was more of a clapped-out Dormobile, took us through the dark, un-festive streets to my hotel while Vicki tried gamely to make small talk.

I was glad to reach the Marco Polo because I was longing for a drink and a wash before meeting up with Liz Rigbey. What a pity the hotel had no knowledge of me or my reservation. But the staff and Vicki, were charming and within half an hour I had the key to room 506 – a suite no less. Hideous, but undeniably a suite, with two bedrooms, a sitting room, hall and bathroom. The decor reminded me of something an aged bachelor uncle would choose, but it was very large and very comfortable.

After ringing Liz and arranging to meet, I had a wash and a small bottle of bubbly, which went straight to my head. Then I met Liz and we headed for the brightly lit restaurant, so bright that the candle on each table seemed entirely superfluous. I noticed that of the sixteen diners, only two were women. Liz told me to have borscht with pancakes and while we ate she gave me the rundown for the following day. She told me that she was hoping it would all go well enough but she was desperate for my help to make the actors gel as a team. Then she said that she had arranged for a guide called Marina to take me on a VIP tour of the Kremlin in the morning. I was so excited by that prospect I could barely concentrate on anything else.

Felicity, the very British interpreter, arrived in time for the main course. She told me how much she loved *The Archers* and Liz told me she was the finest interpreter in Moscow, which I didn't doubt for a second. When it was time to leave, I said my goodnights and arranged to meet up at 9.15 a.m. for breakfast.

The following morning, after a surprisingly good sleep, I met Liz for a morning briefing, and she told me that the problem she was having with the Russian actors was a lack of trust in each other, in her and the project, and a general lack of discipline. Apparently, they found the idea of being punctual, paying attention to each other during read-throughs and generally performing as a team, a complete mystery. So I was to meet them at 3 p.m. and try to convince them that unity is all and that without it they'd fail. Absolutely true.

The walk from the hotel to the studio convinced me what a beautiful, colourful and affluent city London is. I was amazed at the uniform drabness, the broken fences, the gardens of mush and slush and the overwhelming feeling of poverty everywhere in Moscow. We walked past abandoned cars, on broken pavements, through shabby streets where every building seemed to be in need of a full repointing job, let alone a lick of paint. At the office I met my guide, Liz's Russian teacher, Marina, a nice middle-aged lady with perfect English and a sense of humour, and we set off for Red Square. On the way she pointed out several large, dull buildings, of which she seemed genuinely proud, so I played the game and praised them to a fault, when actually I found it all rather depressing. Even at the Kremlin, my heart didn't skip a beat at the beauty of it all, and I couldn't help thinking that the whole place would look so much better under a blanket of crisp white snow. Lenin's tomb was shut for his re-embalming – but Marina assured me he still looked really good!

After a quick look around St Basil's Cathedral, with its extraordinary onion-shaped towers, and a wander round the GUM shopping centre, which reminded me of a prison, it was back to the hotel for lunch. To my dismay, Sacha, my hairy Dormobile driver, was watching television while driving! He had a TV set on the dashboard, aerial up, showing some frantic soap, to which he was constantly glued. It was a relief to reach my hotel in one piece.

At 2.30 Liz, Felicity and I drove to the studio to meet the actors and with the aid of Felicity's interpreting skills, I tried to explain the realities of a radio soap opera and how lucky they were to be involved. I was particularly keen to get over what their commitment should be with regards to punctuality, read-throughs, bringing a pen and making notes and indeed, their commitment to each other. All basic stuff, but they really didn't know. After about an hour we went for a break and I gave them all *Archers'* pens and key rings, which they received as if I had handed them a gift set from Harrods. In return, to my joy, they presented me with a pair of straw slippers and a lovely handwritten note from Tanya, the Judy Bennett of the cast. She was playing the thirteen-year-old, and the card read,

'With our love to you. Thank you. Be healthy, be happy. Tanya Boschkok from farthest Russia.'

I had also brought with me a large bar of Cadbury's Fruit and Nut, which I broke into pieces and handed round. It was as if they had never seen chocolate before, the way they set about devouring it.

After the break, we returned to the studio to continue rehearsing. After a short while one of the female technical staff came in and began talking to the cast in earnest. Although I didn't understand a word, I sensed an atmosphere building up. I asked Felicity if all was well and she told me that the actors were cross and hurt because this woman had, in no uncertain terms, told them their performances were dull, lifeless, rather wooden and not working at all. As you can imagine, the shitsky hit the fansky.

The actors began to shout and one of the actresses ran out of the studio crying her eyes out. Everybody was upset, especially Liz, but eventually, with no little skill, she managed to calm it all down. We all shook hands and then Liz, Felicity and I went off to a reception at the BBC World Service in Moscow.

On the way back to the hotel, we stopped at Liz's office to collect some papers and Liz discovered that one of the principal actors, who the rest couldn't stand, had asked for the next week off – the week in which they were recording episode one! So Liz sacked him and felt a lot better for it. He was an arrogant guy and had been late to my briefing so I wasn't shedding any tears for him either.

The following day Marina arrived at eleven, bearing a bottle of the best vodka and a Moldavian white wine for me to take home. The two together came to $5, then about £3. Cheers!

It was a clear, sunny morning, well below freezing, and we took the trolley bus to Old Arbat Street, which is the Russian version of Petticoat Lane market. I had been warned about pickpockets, thieves and muggers and been told it wasn't safe for foreigners. All I can say is that it was the most uplifting morning anyone could possibly have. This was the part of Moscow to see. Stall after stall lined the long wide street, selling flags, tea sets, samovars, T-shirts, chess sets and all kinds of traditional dolls – *matryoshkas* – some poorly painted, others exquisite. We found a stall of hats and T-shirts, where we chatted and bartered with a young man until I found the hat I really wanted: rabbit fur with ear muffs, the real thing (and only $9, or £6). I put it on and turned to Marina. 'It fits perfectly,' she said. 'You look so Russian!' Indeed I did and I didn't take it off again until I boarded the aircraft.

Everyone had told me I must see the Metro, and I'm so glad I did. The ticket halls are marble, with high ceilings, chandeliers and artwork, and you descend on a clean, fast escalator to an immaculate platform. Every city has something to show off, and Moscow has every reason to be proud of its Metro. So, just as I did with my grandmother years before on the London Underground, Marina and I went two stops, changed, and then came back to where we started. Only Marina wasn't wearing slippers!

A quick lunch at the hotel and then we stopped by the office, on the way to the airport, so I could make my farewells to Liz and all those I had met the day before. The day of the first broadcast was getting ever nearer, deadlines were fast approaching and the place was in chaos, with a last-minute script conference in session. So after a few quick hugs and thank yous, off I went, out into the clear, cold teatime air of Moscow and to the airport. At 6.45 Moscow time, on a crowded 767, I left Russian soil for London and Ambridge, a very contented man.

The soap turned out to be rather a success, with three million listeners and even a guest role for Tony Blair, who played himself on air in 1997. I wonder if they gave *him* a pair of slippers?

When I first joined *The Archers*, Tom Forrest's wife Pru was played by Mary Dalley and, for reasons unknown to me, *it was* decided that Pru wouldn't speak any more. It became a sort of 'in joke'. I don't suppose Mary Dalley found it funny, because you don't get paid unless you speak. Anyway, Pru was referred to quite a lot and never heard, and the public rather liked it. There were frequent letters saying, 'Pru's been very quiet hasn't she?' and indeed, she continued to be so.

In 1989, to celebrate the ten thousandth episode of the programme, it was decided that Pru *should* speak once more. Instead of poor Mary, however, Judi Dench was asked to play Pru and, being a huge fan, she was thrilled. It is remarkable how many famous actors and actresses long to be able to say they've been in *The Archers*. Pru, sadly, never spoke again – probably because they can't afford Dame Judi.

Five years earlier, in 1984, the Duke of Westminster was due to be in the programme to publicize his pet charity, the NSPCC, and he mentioned it to Princess Margaret, who demanded she be included in the episode too. The scene was to be recorded at Kensington Palace, so Arnold Peters and Sara Coward went along with producer William Smethurst and a technical team. Their characters, Jack Woolley and Caroline Bone, were to escort Princess Margaret around a fashion show at Grey Gables, and present her to various people. They rehearsed, with William listening, and when they'd finished the rehearsals William came into the room.

'Ma'am, that was absolutely marvellous,' he said to Princess

Margaret. 'Just one thing,' he continued. 'You're being introduced to the organizers of the Ambridge charity fashion show and everyone is happy – but you sound rather bored.'

She looked at him with a twinkle in her eye and said, 'But I would be, wouldn't I?'

Shortly after my Russian adventure, I was called in to meet Richard Lewis, producer of the BBC game show *Telly Addicts*, hosted by Noel Edmonds. The show had been going for nine years and they wanted to introduce a new side to it, so they wondered if I'd be interested in playing a rather eccentric, old-fashioned scorer. I would be dressed in a dinner jacket and, while keeping the score, do little sketches, to be filmed in crackly black and white, like an old movie. It sounded enormous fun so I accepted immediately. The character I created was a cross between David Jacobs and my father when he was pissed!

Happily it went down well and was popular with the audience so, in the second series, Noel generously suggested that it would be nice to have me in the studio with him, rather than on a separate black and white screen. I moved into colour, no less.

Halfway through the second series, I said to the co-producer, 'I do hope Noel is happy with what I'm doing.'

'Charles,' he replied. 'If he weren't, you wouldn't still be here.'

Noel is an exacting man to work with and a man for whom I have enormous respect. Everybody has read about Noel's success, his wealth, his estates down in Devon and his love of helicopters, but he has a great gift, in that he can identify so well with the man in the street, whether it's on *Telly Addicts* talking to the contestants, *Noel's House Party* or now *Deal or*

No Deal. What's more, he makes it look easy, which is a great talent in itself.

Throughout the series, Noel gained confidence in my ability to shoot from the hip and not be desperately script-bound, so the whole thing got more and more eccentric, I got zanier and the producers gave me wackier things to do, which was fantastic. We did fifty-seven shows together, and never a cross word was spoken. I much enjoyed those years and I'm sorry I haven't worked with him again, but I salute him from afar for what he does on *Deal or No Deal.* Viewers often don't realize that he probably records three shows in one day, so to keep that freshness and sincerity is no mean feat.

During the second series of *Telly Addicts* Richard Lewis created a new series called *Noel's Telly Years*, and he asked me if I would do all the bits that were off camera – the readings, quotations and funny voices. I was delighted, but as this was to be shown on Wednesdays and *Telly Addicts* went out on Mondays, I asked Richard, 'As I'm Charles Collingwood on Monday, can I be somebody else on Wednesday?'

'Oh Charles, for heaven's sake! Who do you want to be?' I could see him getting a bit of a headache.

'Well, I've always thought the two best stage names I've ever seen, I pee into most days of the week,' I answered.

'What are you talking about?' he asked.

'On the credits of *Noel's Telly Years* I want to be the voice of Stelrad Doulton one week, and the next week, I'd like to be the voice of Armitage Shanks.'

'Yes,' he laughed. 'All right.'

The week when I was credited as Armitage Shanks, a representative of the company rang up and asked, 'Who is this actor Armitage Shanks?'

'It's just a stage name,' came the reply. 'And it's quite all right because he's Stelrad Doulton next week.'

'Thank God for that,' they said and left us to get on with it.

FOURTEEN

Sticky Wickets

To a lifelong cricket fanatic, there can be few honours greater than being asked on to *Test Match Special*. In 1995, the year after legendary commentator Brian Johnston died, I was asked to go up to Headingley to be the celebrity guest on the Saturday lunchtime interval. Naturally, I was thrilled.

On the morning of the broadcast I caught an early train from King's Cross and disembarked at Leeds where, to my horror, there appeared to be a three-mile queue for the taxis and buses. The match was due to start in forty minutes and I began to think I'd made a serious misjudgement. Suddenly, I noticed a very neat, dapper, grey-haired man hurrying along in front of me and, from the back, I recognized him as Mike Brearley, the ex-England cricket captain. 'Aha', I thought. 'Whither he goes, I go.'

So I followed Mike Brearley round the corner and straight into the Queen's Hotel. Once inside, I took the bull by the horns. Even though I'd only met him once before, I didn't care, so I greeted him with, 'Mike, how nice to see you.' He rather recoiled because he didn't have a clue who I was, so I introduced myself. He politely shook my hand.

'Charles, how lovely to see you. Are you going to the cricket? Shall we get a taxi together?'

'Yes,' I agreed. 'And I think you should order it.'

He went to the reception desk and asked, very modestly, 'Could we have a taxi for Headingley, please?'

The receptionist picked up the phone, spoke to the taxi company then put his hand over the mouthpiece and said to Mike, 'They say it'll be an hour and twenty minutes.' That was no good so I stepped in.

'Mike, can I make a suggestion? Can you make sure they tell them who it's for?' So Mike told the receptionist who he was.

'It's for Mike Brearley,' said the receptionist into the receiver. Then he put the phone down and said, 'It'll be three minutes.'

We shared a taxi to Headingley and then I sat at the back of the commentary box with all my heroes, Fred Trueman, David 'Bumble' Lloyd, Christopher Martin-Jenkins and Bill Frindall, the famous scorer. It was so exciting. Early on in the day, with the cricket still going on, Christopher Martin-Jenkins came and sat next to me and I saw, in his pile of papers, a sheet which was headed, 'A few facts you ought to know about Charles ...' Curious, I asked what it was.

'You're not supposed to see that,' he replied.

'What?' I protested. 'We're going out live on air. Are you planning any surprises?'

'Go on, then,' he said, handing me the paper and laughing. 'You'd better have a look.'

'A few facts you ought to know about Charles Collingwood' it read. It was a fax, and I looked to see who it was from – *Archers*' editor Vanessa Whitburn. 'Oh Vanessa, for heaven's sake,' I thought. 'You don't need to keep tabs on me the whole time, especially when I'm at the cricket.'

It went on, 'Charles is married to Judy Bennett who plays Shula ...' I thought, 'Everybody knows that.'

'... and he loves cricket ...' Yes. '... and gardening ...'

'This is so boring,' I thought, getting increasingly irritated. Then it read, 'Charles has the largest collection of garden gnomes in northern Europe.'

'Garden gnomes!' I thought. 'Do I?'

And, under the heading 'Little known facts,' it said, 'Charles also ran the marathon in seven-and-a-half hours dressed as a parrot.'

Did I?

Finally it said, 'Charles was the third member of the singing group Mikki and Griff.'

It wasn't from Vanessa at all. It was David Lloyd, who took on the job of England coach a year later. He had taken one look at me and thought, 'He can take a joke.' I still have that fax and it still makes me smile.

At one o'clock, I was on air with Christopher Martin-Jenkins, and he asked me how I had come to love the game of cricket, and then he started eating his sandwich. He knew that once you ask me a question I could take about four hours to answer it, so I told him, 'If you have a father who bowled at you with a tennis ball until it got dark; a housemaster, who was a Cambridge blue, who would bowl at you until you're exhausted, and an old boy of the school who is playing cricket for England; if you have any sort of leaning towards cricket, you're bound to be hooked.'

Then, on air, I told him a story of a visit we had at Sherborne from this famous old boy, the Reverend David Sheppard, who later became the Bishop of Liverpool. As it was the fifties, television and the news media weren't anything like they are today and the only glimpses we had of our cricketing heroes was the occasional picture in a magazine. When we were told this legendary player, who was giving up his life in cricket to become a clergyman, was coming to talk to the colts and the first eleven at Sherborne, I didn't sleep the night before, I was so excited. The moment arrived when we were sitting in a classroom, about thirty of us, and in walked this distinguished young clergyman, with film-star looks, wearing his dog-collar, and for an hour he told us how he had progressed from being a good schoolboy cricketer to Cambridge cricketer, Sussex and then England. He talked about the physical and mental effort it takes to progress from amateur to pro, and it was the most riveting hour. Well, I imagine it was riveting but, tragically, I can't remember a word he said, because he had his fly buttons undone. And when you're fifteen and there's a vicar standing there with his flies undone, you can't do anything but stare agog at this vacant area thinking, 'He's left undone those things that he ought to have done…!'

Back at *Test Match Special*, I was in the commentary box telling this story live on air with Christopher having his lunch, and a few others milling around half-listening to what I was saying. When I said, 'flies undone' you would have thought there had been a small earthquake! The whole room erupted and Christopher nearly choked on his sandwich.

Years later, at the memorial for my old games master Micky Walford, David Sheppard was asked to come and give the blessing, and as we were leaving the chapel, someone asked if I would like to meet him. Would I! To me it was like meeting a film star! Sure enough, there was this distinguished ex-cricketing bishop standing at the top of the chapel steps.

'David,' said our mutual acquaintance, 'I'd like you to meet Charles Collingwood. He's Brian in *The Archers*.'

The Right Reverend David Sheppard clutched the crucifix round his neck, took a deep intake of breath and said, 'We don't like *you* at all.'

'You'd better meet my wife, Judy then,' I replied. 'She plays Shula.'

At which he opened his arms and said, 'Ah, but we *love* you.'

When Judy and I were doing our stage show in Chester some time later, we were having a pub lunch and in walked David Sheppard and his wife Grace. By then, he was in his early seventies and in remission from cancer. He was looking at the blackboard at the specials when I approached him and bravely called him David. He looked at me in amazement, as if to say, 'Who is this person?'

I reminded him of who we were and the four of us spent an hour having a lovely lunch, chatting about old times and cricket.

A few months later we were invited to do our show again in Chester, this time in aid of a cancer charity, so I wrote to David and asked him if he and Grace would like to come. To my great joy they came with a group of friends, and it was a special thrill to see my boyhood hero throwing his head back and laughing. 'After all the pleasure you've given me over the years,' I thought. 'This is payback time.'

Sadly, all too soon, the cancer returned and, after a courageous fight, David Sheppard, the bishop and my cricketing hero, died in 2005.

As I related on *Test Match Special*, due to my father's enthusiasm for the sport, I was a keen cricketer from an early age. While I was at RADA, whenever time allowed, I was playing cricket quite seriously for a number of clubs, including the Hampshire Hogs. One weekend, the Hogs had a two-day match at the St Cross ground in Winchester, and I had a purple day. It just so happened that the great Harry (H.S.) Altham, who had been president of the MCC, was watching me and when the match finished, he approached me.

'I like the look of the way you were playing today, Charles,' he said. 'Why don't you pop down to Southampton so we can have a better look at you to see if you'd fit in where Hampshire's concerned.'

I was hugely flattered, but I knew I wasn't nearly good enough to be a professional, so I said, 'I'm sorry Mr Altham, but I'm going to be an actor.'

And I'm very glad I did because I would never have made it. At that time, of course, I didn't know if I was good enough to earn a living as an actor, but it happily proved to be more lucrative than if I had decided to be a cricketer.

At twenty I was lucky enough to be elected a playing member of the MCC, which meant I had access to the facilities at Lord's, including the nets. During those dark years of my unemployment when I was cleaning people's houses and working in shops, my self-esteem wasn't at its best. All my peers were finding success and moving on and I didn't seem to be achieving much, but come the summer I would find myself on a bus going up Baker Street through St John's Wood to Lord's.

In those days, as a playing member you could turn up at any time and say, 'I'd like somebody to bowl at me in the nets please,' and the MCC would phone down to the young professionals, who would come and do just that. It was a members' privilege and half a dozen young pros of my age or younger would come along and bowl to me for however long I wanted. Then one of them would bat and I would join the rest of them in the bowling. Afterwards, having had a shower, I'd get on the bus thinking, 'At least, I can do something quite well.'

On one occasion, Yorkshire were practising in the nets in preparation for a match against Middlesex the following day, and Richard Hutton, the son of the legendary England cricket captain Len Hutton, was batting. Somehow I found myself bowling at Richard, who by then was playing for Yorkshire and England, and to my amazement and delight, I knocked his middle stump out of the ground. He didn't say 'well bowled', he didn't even look at me, he just said, 'Fuck it!' and put the stump back up.

That's the difference between enjoying yourself as an amateur and having to get it right as a pro, whether you're an actor or a sportsman.

In order to become a 'playing' member of the MCC I was required, just as today, to play a number of qualifying matches for the club. In one of my qualifiers we played against Stroud in Gloucestershire, and my parents came to watch. I was very surprised that Tony Lewis of Glamorgan and England was in the same team as me. Tony couldn't get a run for his county that year, he had no form and his confidence had gone, so he dropped himself from the Glamorgan team and was getting some practice by playing a match for MCC. He was promptly dropped, first ball, before making a glittering hundred in about an hour. He oozed class and was head and shoulders above than the rest of us.

When it was our turn to field, I opened the bowling with Tony standing by my side at mid-off and he treated me as if I was his opening bowler for Glamorgan, not just a young actor who was bowling in a match for the MCC. He's a good man and it's always a privilege when I meet him socially at Lord's.

Over the years I've played for so many clubs but my proudest boast is that I am now President of the Stage Cricket Club, a club for actors, which I played for over a period of four decades. We are not like the Lord's Taverners, a celebrity team, but more akin to the serious wandering cricket clubs that play over forty fixtures a year to quite a high standard.

My first game for the Stage was against a bank side in south London and naturally I was very nervous. The captain was John Slater who, at the time, was the star of the television series *Z Cars* and had been a star for many years. Edward Cast, a fine actor who went on to become well known for playing Mike Nash in *Waggoner's Walk*, was also playing. When I was asked to bowl my first over for the Stage, I was determined to make a showing of it, to make an impression, and as I measured out my run, Ted Cast came over and said, 'If you get a wicket in this over, darling, I'll give you a Spangle.' And I thought, 'Well, I've never played cricket with anybody who's called me darling before, or been offered Spangles!'

Suffice it to say I got two wickets in that over and got two Spangles, and dear old Ted always had a pocketful of Spangles to hand out to high achievers.

Before I joined, Brian, now Lord, Rix was also a member of the Stage CC. Watching cricket at Lord's once, we were chatting about his career and the Whitehall farces with which he had been so closely connected, and he told me that his company were so familiar with each other and their performances that they used to meet on stage every evening and just launch straight in. One summer afternoon John Slater, who was also appearing in the farce, was playing a midweek game for the Stage but Brian had a meeting, so couldn't play. That evening, Brian walked on stage to do his first scene with John and one other actor; Brian was in the middle, John was on his right and the other actor was on his left. What Brian didn't know was that, early in the match, John had been hit in the eye by the cricket ball and had spent most of the afternoon in hospital having it stitched up so, by the time he made his entrance, his eye was the size of a cricket ball itself. As Brian turned to deliver his first line to John he was faced with the sight of this huge shiner and John's deadpan expression. Then he turned to the other actor on his left who hadn't told him that he'd been stung in the mouth by a wasp. 'Both my fellow actors had vast swellings all over their faces,' he told me. 'I couldn't get the words out, I was laughing so much.'

Yes, we Stage cricketers are a dedicated bunch. We had one actor, David Purcell, who was in summer season in Sidmouth, in Devon, and he turned up one Sunday at Cheam for a match. He'd finished the show the night before and although he was opening in a new play back in Devon on the Monday, he'd driven up through the night to play cricket that afternoon. It was a miserable, drizzly day, but the team arrived at Cheam, I won the toss and we batted. David opened the batting, he was immediately out for nought, and then the rain came down and we never bowled another ball. The game was cancelled, and we all watched him get in his little Ford Prefect with the lines for the new play on the passenger seat beside him, desperately trying to get them in his head before the opening night, as he set off on the long drive back to Sidmouth. That's dedication to cricket.

When I first joined the Stage Cricket Club, it was my job as a junior member of the team to get the sides together. This entailed sitting by the side of the phone with a list of players, ringing each one to find out if they were available for the following Sunday or the midweek game on a Wednesday.

On one particular occasion, on the morning of a match at Richmond in Surrey, I had almost exhausted the extensive list and was still a player short. The one remaining name was that of the famous actor and playwright Harold Pinter, a passionate cricketer with his own side, The Gaieties. 'Oh well,' I thought, 'nothing ventured, nothing gained. I've rung everybody else. I'll try Harold Pinter.'

It was just before nine in the morning, so I dialled the number and the phone at the other end rang and rang until, eventually, a deep gruff voice, half asleep, answered, 'Hello?'

'Hello. Harold Pinter?' I ventured.

'Yes.'

'This is Charles Collingwood from the Stage Cricket Club. I wondered if you'd be free to play cricket against Richmond this afternoon?'

And, rather surprisingly *without* a pause, he said, 'Fuck off!' and he put the phone down.

Tragically, as far as my career goes, those are the only two words Harold Pinter ever said to me.

In early September every year, the Stage plays at Lord's cricket ground against the Cross Arrows, a fixture I have enjoyed for many years. Indeed I'm also a member of the Cross Arrows, and one of the few outsiders, because it's mainly a club made up of people who work at Lord's for the whole of the summer, which includes the Middlesex team, the ground staff, right down to the girls who print the programmes.

Apparently, over a hundred years ago when the club was founded, the team was getting into a coach to travel to a match and somebody asked, 'Where are we playing today?' The captain pointed north and said ''Cross 'arrow way,' meaning towards Harrow. From that day forth the team was called the Cross Arrows.

During one match for the Cross Arrows, when I was in my early fifties, I was standing in the slips with some of the young pros and they said, 'Come on, Charles, let's play slip roulette.'

'What the hell's that?' I asked.

'We're in the slips, and you're first slip so you shut your eyes and we cover for you, so if the ball comes your way we try and catch it. Second ball, second slip shuts his eyes and we cover for him and third ball, the third slip shuts his eyes. The reason it's called "slip roulette" is because if it comes your way and we miss, you'll get it in the teeth.'

'Do you mind if I pass on this?' I demurred. 'I don't think my agent will quite understand if I lose all my teeth and can't work tomorrow.'

As well as being an actor, it has been my great pleasure to take part in some wonderful panel games, including *Just a Minute, Countdown* and *Call My Bluff*. The first time I appeared on *Call My Bluff*, in 1995, Judy and I had just been to the Far East to do an Alan Ayckbourn play called *Relatively Speaking*. While we were in Bangkok we had more clothes made for two people than is truly decent, because tailor-made clothes were beautifully made and incredibly cheap. The *Call My Bluff* recording was the week after I returned and, as it was TV rather than radio, I thought carefully about what I should wear. I'd bought this marvellous black silk, zip-up jacket, so I wore it with a black-and-gold silk scarf, black silk trousers and black shoes. 'That's the outfit,' I thought. 'That'll wow them.'

The show was recorded at Pebble Mill so I arrived on the day and I was introduced to Sandi Toksvig, my captain, and Trevor McDonald, the other member of our team. The opposite captain was Alan Coren, an absolute hero of mine, but I didn't get a chance to meet him before we started the show. I sort of waved at him, then we went into the studio and there sat the chairman, Bob Holness, in between the two teams. We all got miked up and I was nervous because while I was looking across at my hero, Alan Coren, I was actually sitting next to the bitingly witty Sandi. Just before the music started, the studio manager was counting down in front of the large audience, and Alan, staring at me in my black-and-gold silk scarf and my black silk zip-up with black silk trousers, leant across from the other table and, in a loud voice, said, 'Charles, why have you come dressed as a rear gunner?' I was still laughing when it was my turn to do the first word.

Subsequently, I was fortunate to be asked to appear quite regularly, on Alan's team as well as Sandi's. My proudest moment was when I had to describe the word *Koeksister*, and I had the true definition – the South African word for a doughnut. I took a bag of doughnuts with me and hid them under the table, and when it was my time to do *Koeksister*, I got out my bag of doughnuts, and Bob Holness went into a terrible panic, wondering what the hell I was going to do. I handed them round and everyone tucked in, getting sugar all round their mouths, while I gave my description, 'And it's a South African doughnut and it's called *Koeksister* because it was a family that discovered it and as the little boy who had made them, opened the oven door, he took them out, turned to the young girl on his right and said, 'would you like a koek sister?' (cake, sister. Got it?)

Another funny memory of *Call My Bluff* is with Nicky Campbell, who was at that time cutting his teeth on Radio 5 and just breaking into television. Although a natural broadcaster, he can sometimes be a bit too smart for his own good ... Nicky was on Sandi's team and I was with Michael Buerk and Alan.

One of the definitions I had was for a nineteenth-century word 'nammet' which means 'a light meal' and, according to the information I was given, Thomas Hardy used it in *Return of the Native*, which of course I mentioned in my explanation.

It was Nicky's turn to guess and, after dismissing Michael Buerk rather brusquely, he turned to me and said, 'Charles, I have read every word that Hardy wrote, and that word was never in one of his books, so it's rubbish.'

And he turned to Alan, and said, 'So it's you who's telling the truth.' Alan revealed 'Bluff' and I happily picked up my 'True' card.

'Nicky, there is just *one* word of Thomas Hardy you haven't read.'

FIFTEEN

Laughter and Intrigue

In the early 1990s, I received a call from a rather panic-stricken woman in need of our help. 'I've organized a speaker for a book festival at the University College School in Hampstead for this coming Sunday,' she told me. 'I've sold 200 tickets and he's pulled out. Can you help me?'

At that time, I was slightly involved with the North London Hospice and occasionally I would go in and talk to the patients and tell them some funny stories, which was certainly fulfilling for me and, I hope, of some help to them. The flustered lady was Pauline Treen, who was in charge of fund-raising for the hospice, so I was all too willing to do what I could.

'I'll ring you back,' I said. I put the phone down and turned to Judy, 'You know we were going away for the weekend? Well, we're not any more. On Sunday we've got to do forty minutes for the North London Hospice.'

For some time we had felt we ought to have a go at putting together a show as husband and wife, because we weren't aware of any other married couples spending their lives in the same soap opera. As you may have gathered, I really am relentlessly anecdotal and as I had been giving after-dinner speeches for years, I thought, 'We'll do it together and I'll give Judy some of my anecdotes – not the good ones of course!'

The following Sunday we turned up, talked for forty minutes and it seemed to go well.

Shortly after the hospice performance, we were asked to go

to the Far East to perform in the Alan Ayckbourn play *Relatively Speaking*, and while we were there we realized how intrigued the audience were to watch a real-life husband and wife playing a completely different married couple in the play. It's not unique. From years back couples like Jack Hulbert and Cicely Courtneidge, Michael Denison and Dulcie Gray and Judi Dench and Michael Williams have worked together, but we have the extra aspect of being in *The Archers* so, on our return from the Far East, we decided to get a proper show together and look for a promoter.

That's when Clive Conway, who puts on one-man shows and *Evenings with* ... came on board. He's an accomplished musician so he invited us to the Chesterfield Theatre, where he entertained with his musicians in the first half and we performed in the second. We called the show *Laughter and Intrigue* principally because we felt the audience were intrigued to see a married couple perform, and laughter because, thankfully, that's what happened most evenings. In the early stages we were fortunate to have the assistance of a very distinguished theatre director, Clifford William, late of the RSC no less. Neither Judy nor I had worked with Clifford before, and he guided us, helped us put the show together then came up to Chesterfield and watched it. The only note he gave us afterwards was, 'My dears, you have a jewel, go out and enjoy it.' We had Clifford to thank for creating that jewel.

Over the next few years, throughout the late 1990s, Clive proceeded to get us date after date around the country, and by the time we called it a day we had performed over 150 times, from Thurso to the Scilly Isles. We decided from the outset that if we were going to tour round the country we would plan to stay a night or two in each area, so that we could get to see more of this beautiful island of ours. *Laughter and Intrigue* enabled us to explore the country from top to bottom over a period of five or six years.

We had plenty of laughs along the way and suffered some wonderful put-downs too. At one venue in the Midlands, I was a little apprehensive as we drove through the local area because it looked fairly unsavoury. I felt I'd be lucky if my precious car still had wheels by the time we finished later that evening. As we entered the complex, the first thing I noticed was the smell of chlorine, and in the distance I could hear the thwack of squash balls and I realized that we were in a massive sports centre and, somewhere in there, was a vast black dungeon where we were due to perform.

As we walked into this huge hall, to set up for the show, the man who'd booked us came in and, without saying 'Hello,' he shook me by the hand and said, 'We've never had the spoken word here before!'

Later that evening, we performed in a 400-seater, in front of about forty willing souls, and at the end, as we were signing autographs, the same man came up to the table and, with a beaming smile, said, 'If I'd known it was going to be like that I'd have told people!'

Hey ho, I just hope he didn't get an Arts Council Grant.

We performed once as a breakfast entertainment at a hotel in Windsor, and as the man was laying out the tables and putting up our stage in the dining room, he remarked, rather disparagingly, 'We open the doors for boxing.' Obviously, by opening the doors you can get a larger audience, which to him we clearly didn't warrant.

At one venue in Essex, the organizer said, 'Now look, you haven't got a big audience tonight, but there are only twelve people who can read in this part of Essex, and I want you to know they're all coming!'

In Wales we were in a huge 300-seater but I felt early on that there weren't many people in: you can sense an empty house. After about fifteen minutes, Judy had a solo section, the lights were dimmed and she was in a spotlight, so I though I'd count the number of people in the audience – it didn't take long. There were thirty-three and afterwards, as we signed autographs, one woman came up and demanded rather aggressively, 'Why have you come here tonight?'

'Oh please,' I beseeched. 'Spare us that. What do you mean?'

'Well,' she said. 'Why have they booked you on the night of the local eisteddfod?' It gave us a little hope that at least some of the 5,000 culture lovers that were up the road at the eisteddfod might have come to see our show had it been on another evening.

By and large, however, we had wonderful audiences, many full houses and a tremendous reaction. We were very mindful of the BBC ruling that at no time were we allowed to play our *Archers*' characters onstage, although we could refer to them. We would always instruct the organizers that, when publicizing the event, they could not advertise, 'Brian and Shula in *Laughter and Intrigue*', but would always have to put Charles Collingwood and Judy Bennett, and underneath in brackets they could mention our character names.

In every venue they got it right, except on one occasion when we drove into the town and there was a huge banner across the main High Street, which read, 'Brian and *Sheila* in *Laughter and Intrigue*'. What can you do?

Perhaps the most memorable evening was in the Scilly Isles. A number of years earlier, when Chris Evans and Gaby Roslin were presenting *The Big Breakfast* on Channel 4, Tamsin Greig and I were asked to be early morning surprise guests. Every week, they invited a family on the show as studio guests and they would ask which celebrities they would most like to meet. Much to Channel 4's amazement, one family from the Scilly Isles asked to meet Brian and Debbie from *The Archers*, and so at about half past five in the morning we turned up at the studio. I took Jane, who was twelve, along with me and although she enjoyed it, she recoiled in horror because one of the other guests that morning was a man who had a nest of spiders in his ear! Jane has a slight thing about spiders, so it didn't get her day off to a good start.

Anyway, there I was with Tamsin and Chris Evans, hiding behind the kitchen on the *Big Breakfast* set, and all of a sudden we popped up and went 'Surprise, surprise,' in front of the guests, Kristine Tayler and her lovely family. When the show was over I was having a cup of coffee with Kris and I told her I'd never been to the Scilly Isles.

A year or two later, being a huge *Archers*' fan, Kris heard about *Laughter and Intrigue* and organized for us to do our show on St Mary's, the principal island of the Scillies. She arranged our accommodation and travel and we stayed on the lovely island of Bryher, where she has her home. On the night of the show Judy and I went over on the ferry to St Mary's and Kris told us that all the outlying islands, like Tresco, St Martin's and St Agnes, were virtually closing down for the evening because the entire population were coming to the show.

Half an hour before curtain up, one of the organizers asked, 'When it's over, if you could be as quick as possible with your props etc., because the boat that's taking you back to Bryher at 10.15 is the same boat that's taking the audience back to Bryher, so they'll be waiting.'

After the show, with a few helping hands, we packed up as quickly as possible and ran down to the ferry. We boarded the ferry to a generous round of applause, and then a large box of fish and chips was produced. As we took the twenty-minute trip back to Bryher, we all ate fish and chips with our fingers before going to the pub where we drank long into the night. What an evening it was!

My favourite memory of the ferry trip was Kris Tayler saying 'Now you see that gentleman over there? You should be very honoured.'

'Why?' I asked.

'Well, we haven't seen him in shoes for twelve years!'

I just had to meet this guy so I sauntered over and said, 'How do you do?'

'How do you do?' he said, and with a very strong accent. 'Do you know, youse a lot nicer on the stage than you ares on the wireless. I don't like you on the wireless, you'm a bit of a bounder.'

'I'm afraid that's the part I play,' I explained and I started telling him how much I loved the Scilly Isles. As I spoke, I could hear myself sounding more and more patronizing and pompous and saying things like, 'It strikes me it's just like it was when I was a boy. You don't need to lock up, it feels so safe, I'm sure there can be no crime,' and so on.

He was looking at me with twinkly, blue eyes, not saying a word. When I'd finished, he nodded.

'Ju know, Charles,' he said. 'What you sez is true, because I can tell you, I hasn't eaten a child for ten year!' And then he looked at me and added, 'No, I correct myself. I's wrong – I had half a one because I could keep him in the cool box.'

Talk about putting me in my place!

Occasionally, some people got rather overexcited at the prospect of our show, particularly in a small community like a village, because it seemed a big event. One lady organizer was so eager, as we told her about our entrance, how it started with the music, that we would perform for about an hour, and I instructed her, 'The interval will be fifteen minutes but you'll have to get all the audience back in and make sure you tell us, so we can come on for the second half.'

'Of course I will,' she nodded enthusiastically.

What we didn't know was that as soon as the first half started, she relaxed, and when the interval came she couldn't get to the wine quick enough. Judy and I were relaxing in our dressing room, my jacket slumped on the back of the chair, Judy with her shoes off and her slippers on, when to our horror our play-on music started: the woman had completely forgotten to tell us that everybody was ready for the second half. We had a little more 'play-on' music than usual that evening!

Every time we did the show we had a set routine, getting in, setting up, going to the dressing room, having a little sleep, rehearsing a few bits, particularly our opening, which was a clever verse of rhyming couplets, written especially for us by Richard Stilgoe.

After rehearsing, we would get into our performance clothes – they weren't costumes as such – ready to do the show at the appointed hour. One filthy September night in Barrow-in-Furness, ten minutes before curtain up at 8 p.m., we were in the dressing room. Judy was completely ready for the show, except she still had her slippers on, and I asked, 'When are you going to put your high heels on?' (Actually, one of the reasons I enjoyed doing the show was that Judy has quite the best legs I've ever seen, but she will wear trousers, and the only time I ever got a really good look at them was when she did the stage show and wore a short skirt and high heels!) At the mention of heels, her hand went up to her mouth.

'Oh my God,' she said. 'I haven't got them!' By now, it's eight minutes to eight o'clock.

'Where the hell are they?' I said.

'They're back at the B&B.'

There was no time for me to say 'You stupid woman. Why can't you remember ...' They had to be fetched. I tore out of the dressing room shouting, 'Tell the company manager.' I ran out of the stage door to my car, which was parked up against the glass-fronted foyer, and I could see most of our audience finishing off their glasses of wine.

I could also see the front-of-house manager just behind the glass. In my moment of anxiety I thought I'll bang on the glass to let him know he'll have to hold the curtain while I get Judy's shoes, so with a frantic expression on my face I went bang, bang, bang, bang on the glass – and the one person who didn't hear me was him. The audience did, and what they saw was one half of the act they'd paid money to be entertained by, banging on the glass like a madman, then mouthing 'oh bollocks!' and getting in his car and driving off in the pouring rain.

But there was nothing I could do. I whizzed down the road, I wanted to break the speed limit but, would you believe it, I had to go past a police station. I got to the B&B in about four minutes, left the car running, ran upstairs and trashed the room looking for these shoes, which I found in one of the drawers (I now know why burglars never shut drawers!). I grabbed them, ran downstairs and, as I was getting in the car, another car was coming in the gate, so I went up to the window and I barked, 'Park there, now!' This poor woman shot her car into the drive in terror, I got in my car, whizzed back to the theatre, and it was one minute past eight when I got back and gave the shoes to Judy. My heart was beating like mad, so it was a relief to find the company manager in our dressing room saying, 'It's all right. Don't worry, we have a few wheelchairs in this evening so we're having to hold the curtain three or four minutes anyway, get your breath back.'

Being the people we are, we then found it funny, in fact we were laughing so much we didn't know how we were going to get on stage. But we did, and the odd thing was that in our customary question-and-answer session at the end of the show, there was no reference to my banging on the window. Perhaps they thought it hadn't really happened, just some apparition that happens in Barrow-in-Furness on a wet night.

Before one show in Boston, Lincolnshire, we were told that the Archers Anarchists had been threatening to disrupt it. We have our own fan club, called the Archers Addicts, but there's also a spin-off called the Archers Anarchists, a group of people who believe that *The Archers* is, in fact, a fly-on-the-wall documentary. In my opinion, they all need medication, but we'd been warned that they had been threatening to gatecrash the stage and announce, 'Ladies and gentlemen, this is all rubbish, they *are* Brian and Shula, don't believe they are actors,' or some such nonsense.

We were slightly unnerved, but the theatre staff reassured us that these so-called Anarchists wouldn't interrupt the show, which they didn't. However, they did get in and put some literature on each seat of the theatre, purporting to the fact that we weren't who we said we were – and it didn't help the first twenty-minutes of the show. There was a certain tension in the air before the audience realized all would be well with no unwelcome disturbances.

All good things have to come to an end. After five or six years we were driving in my car and Judy had the AA book on her lap. I noticed she was flicking through the pages, and all of a sudden she piped up, 'Do you realize we've appeared on every page in this book?' I felt in that instant that our show together was over, she'd had enough.

Judy had never really enjoyed *Laughter and Intrigue* as much as I did. She's what I call a 'proper actor' and, like most actors, she enjoys hiding behind a character, so being herself, in her own clothes, on stage in front of as many as a thousand people, terrifies her. It terrifies me too, but in a much more constructive way. I can handle it and once I'm out there I enjoy every minute of it. But, hand on heart, I know that Judy continued to do *Laughter and Intrigue* long after she wanted to finish it. She did it for my sake because she knew that there was a market out there, but all of a sudden she'd had enough. I totally understood, and that's why I'm happy to do my own show, without her.

I miss her. I miss the fact that she always had two coughs during our show – one to signify, 'You're going on too long,' and I used to hear that quite often; the other cough, which was a little more frantic, meant 'You've left out a large chunk,' which was much more worrying. Now, when I'm doing the show and she's out front, I still listen out for those coughs.

For many years I played cricket with a dear friend, an actor named Nigel Miles-Thomas. When he was younger, he looked like a handsome Sylvester Stallone, which meant plenty of welcome attention from the girls. In fact, he thought monogamy was what you make dining room tables out of! However, he did marry a Canadian girl called Natalie Bohm, who had been to Oxford, but then took a drama course in Los Angeles, having decided she wanted to be an actress. Her parents, who were very wealthy, set up a production company for her. Her family had a home in Hong Kong and she and Nigel, very successfully, took plays to the Far East and put them on at a number of ex-pat clubs in Hong Kong, Singapore and Bangkok.

After-dinner speakers there were two a penny, but actually

seeing a play that had recently been on in the West End, as long as it only had a small cast and was perhaps abridged to be slightly shorter, was the sort of entertainment they were only too happy to have after a meal.

Nigel was keen to take the Alan Ayckbourn comedy, *Relatively Speaking* over there, and one day he said, 'Charles, it's a four-hander, and you and Judy are absolutely perfect for the parts of Philip and Sheila.'

Neither of us had been on stage for a number of years – Judy for thirty years and me for ten – and the idea of learning a play again required a few deep breaths, so for some time we funked it. Nigel, bless his heart, eventually made us an offer which, in every way financially and otherwise, we simply couldn't refuse. I asked if I could choose the director, and he agreed.

Years earlier, when we'd done *The Archers'* show in Newbury, where a number of the cast were going onstage for the first time in years, we had a director called Patrick Tucker who had worked a lot at the Royal Shakespeare Company and was also teaching at drama schools. I'd enjoyed working with Patrick and I felt that, being a teacher, he was just the right person to help Judy rekindle her stage technique, and so it proved. He put on a wonderful production of *Relatively Speaking*, but I am eternally grateful for the one-to-one help he gave Judy during the weeks of rehearsal, which culminated, as I hoped it would, in Judy giving a tremendous performance as Sheila. In some early performances she was undoubtedly anxious, but it wasn't long before she was flying: in fact, I have to say, she was rather funnier than I wanted her to be! However, there was one performance which was the most terrifying that Judy and I have ever given.

Patrick wasn't able to come to the Far East so, naturally, as the director, he wanted to see a full performance before we left.

As I've said, I was involved with the North London Hospice, so it occurred to me that we could do a fund-raising performance and, because Toby and Barney had been at Highgate School, they kindly let us use their theatre. A sixth-former at the school called David Babani, who was crazy about the theatre in every aspect, helped us on the night with the stage management, the lighting and the sound effects and was truly committed. No wonder he now runs The Chocolate Factory Theatre in London with such success.

On the night, it suddenly occurred to Judy and myself that the audience would include not only people we'd known for many years, but also a number of parents whose children I had criticized at various school drama competitions over the years. Now they were about to get their chance to say, 'Let's see how bloody good you are.' So by the time the show was due to start, we were shaking.

The first scene was played by Nigel and Natalie, then there was a lighting change, a quick scene change, and there Judy and I sat, as Philip and Sheila, on the stage having breakfast. I could sense how nervous Judy was and three lines into the scene she dried stone dead. Not a line. Not a word. If somebody dries, most actors can picture the page in their heads, and I could see the page, I just couldn't see her line, so I came in with a line of my own. It wasn't actually the next line, it was about three lines later, but it didn't matter. Judy picked up the cue and she never dried again. But it was a nervous moment, and one that all actors will identify with.

In that first scene, I slipped in an *Archers'* gag, which worked extremely well. After a long pause, having our coffee and reading our Sunday papers, Philip just says, 'Sheila ...' and I suggested to Patrick, 'Because of who we play in *The Archers*, could I get away with saying "Shula – er sorry, Sheila ..."'

'Yes, go on, do it!' he agreed.

So I did, every night, starting at Highgate, and then in the Far East, I would make my deliberate mistake and the audience would first gasp, then laugh, and quite often they'd clap as well. It was naughty, but it worked, so apologies to Alan Ayckbourn.

We progressed to the Far East and had an amazing month performing in some wonderful clubs. The Bohms were extremely generous and gave us a whole floor of their glorious apartment in Hong Kong. From there, we flew to Singapore, which was great fun, and then we were due to fly from Singapore to Bangkok. I kept asking Nigel 'Are we flying BA to Bangkok?'

'Yes, yes, we are,' he assured me.

On the morning of the flight we were in the rooftop pool of our hotel in Singapore, and again I repeated my question, 'Just checking now. We are flying BA aren't we?'

'Yes, yes, BA,' he answered but there was something about the way he said 'yes' that made me question him further.

'You do mean British Airways, don't you?'

'Ah,' he said. 'Until now you've only asked if it was BA.'

'Well, yes. Come on then, what does BA stand for?' I enquired.

'Biman Airlines.'

'Who the hell are they?'

'Bangladesh Airways.'

'Oh God!' I thought.

Now, I'm not wishing to cast aspersions on Biman Airlines, and neither should I, because after a huge lengthy queue, where I refused to go on this vast plane to Bangkok with people sitting with chickens in cages on their knees, I put in for an upgrade. I told the man at the desk that my wife and I were very famous actors from Britain and I wanted us to be upgraded and, to my delight, we all got seats in the premium class. We boarded a beautiful, comfortable plane, quaffed mango juice before we took off and Biman Airlines flew us to Bangkok for the final leg of our journey.

SIXTEEN

An Affair to Remember

From the time of Brian's dalliance with Caroline Bone, right up until the end of the 1990s, women throughout the land accosted me with the same question, 'When is Brian going to have another affair?'

The answer came out of the blue. It was the summer of 2001 and Judy and I had just got back from the Edinburgh Festival, where we had been doing our stage show. *The Archers'* editor Vanessa Whitburn phoned and told me that Brian was going to have an affair with Siobhan Hathaway, the doctor's wife.

'I think this will satisfy them, Charles,' she said. 'It's not just going to be an affair, it's going to be a love affair. But Brian's not going to leave Jennifer.'

Not only was I grateful to Vanessa for creating this storyline, but I was hugely relieved, too, because if Brian left Jennifer the likelihood is that he'd have to leave Ambridge, which would mean a few months fun and then no pay. Is it worth it?

'Tell me more,' I said.

Vanessa went on to explain that Brian was going to fall for Siobhan, but would not stop loving Jennifer: he would love both women hugely, but in different ways. Brian would continue to live at home and it would all be divine to start with. Brian would revel in it: Siobhan was younger, sexier and more vibrant than his wife, but Jennifer would still be running the home and looking after the family. At that time Vanessa didn't tell me that they were going to have a child and Brian would finally get the little boy he wanted.

A few weeks later, Siobhan and Brian started the on-air affair in a hotel in Amsterdam. It all started when Brian became a shoulder for Siobhan to cry on. One evening he popped round to Siobhan's house with a bottle of wine to talk about something happening in the village, and sensed some unhappiness in her marriage, and he thought, 'Hang on, there's a vulnerable woman here who might like the advice of an older man,' and took the opportunity to suggest another meeting and another bottle of wine.

Siobhan was an interpreter so when she mentioned she was going to Amsterdam to do some work, Brian seized his chance and told her, 'It would be nice if we could meet there, wouldn't it?' Brian was about to visit his property in Hungary, so he arranged to fly back via Amsterdam and spent the night with Siobhan.

Unlike the affair with Caroline, which was mostly in restaurants, a lot of the action happened in the backs of taxis, so there was much heavy breathing, and 'this shouldn't be happenings' and 'Ooh, Brian, ooh, stop it Brians', and 'Siobhan, I can't live with out yous'.

The writing was so good, and it was such fun to play. Brian was thoroughly enjoying himself, juggling sixteen glass balls in the air and getting away with it.

Then Siobhan dropped the bombshell: 'I'm pregnant. I'm going to have a baby.' When Brian found out that it was the boy he'd always longed for he was in a quandary and Siobhan was convinced he would leave Jenny.

Rauiri was born in November 2002, but nobody in Ambridge knew who the father was and, if it came up in conversation, Brian would say, 'I don't know anything about it and I couldn't care less who the father is.'

Just before Christmas there was a huge showdown, when

Debbie found out what her father had been up to. Thrilled with little Rauiri, in one father, mother and son scene, Brian had produced his handkerchief to wipe up a little bit of baby sick, and Siobhan took it to have it washed. Later, Debbie saw Siobhan holding the handkerchief with Brian's monogram, and the penny dropped.

There was one scene between Brian and Debbie that was about ten minutes long. Brian came home late at night and was surprised to find Debbie waiting up for him and he said, 'Hello, darling. You're up late.'

'Dad. I know.'

'Know what?'

'I know.'

It was the most fantastic scene and beautifully written with some wonderful lines. At one point Debbie says, 'Then she got pregnant.'

'Yes,' replies Brian incredulously. 'I don't know how.'

'The usual way I would imagine!' spits Debbie.

To have such good dialogue and to play the scene with Tamsin was fantastic. The critics loved it – and Ned Sherrin even compared it to Chekhov. The storyline was the highpoint of my *Archers*' career. It was as good as it can get for me.

Debbie insisted Brian told Jennifer, which inevitably led to more great scenes. When Brian told Jennifer, she – Angela Piper – went berserk. Angie picked a knife off the table, and she was so convincing I actually had to back away. I remember thinking, 'Don't take this too far, darling, will you?' I had visions of that thing being plunged into my stomach. It would make great radio, but there would only be one take!

The person who was really given the chance to come out of her shell was Holly Chapman, who plays Brian's youngest daughter. Playing Alice, Holly hadn't always been much challenged, because the character was just a little girl with everyday dialogue. But when Alice found out her father was having the affair with Siobhan and that Rauiri was his son, Holly had some pretty demanding scenes that went way beyond the usual, 'Hello, Dad, can you pass me the cornflakes?' Holly more than delivered, and proved what a superlative actress she is.

By now, Brian had dropped every one of the glass balls he'd been juggling, they'd all smashed to bits and he was desperately trying to cover his tracks. Siobhan was saying, 'Come away with me,' and he soothed her with promises, but he had no intention of losing the 2,000-acre farm and the homely comforts of his wife. He did love Siobhan, but she was in her thirties, he was sixty and he wasn't going to give up his comfortable lifestyle. He still loved Jennifer and, even though she was giving him a terrible time, he knew she hadn't done anything wrong.

Eventually, Siobhan took Rauiri to Ireland and Brian tried to put things right at Home Farm, but for a long time the atmosphere was pretty frosty. The most amazing aspect to me, though, was the reaction of the British people, particularly the women. Within a month of Jenny finding out and being absolutely livid, some were beginning to say to me, 'I think Jennifer's being a bit heavy over this, don't you? It's time she got over it.'

Excuse me! He not only had an affair that lasted over a year, it also resulted in a little boy. And you think it's time that she got over it? I couldn't believe it.

Siobhan returned to Ambridge, expecting Brian to drop everything and come back with her to Ireland but, while they were out in the car, he broke the news to her that he was not leaving. She went mad and tried to end it all by grabbing the steering wheel out of his hands. They had the most appalling crash and that was how the episode ended, with Siobhan climbing out of the wreck of a car saying, 'Oh, Brian, what have I done?' Nothing from him. To the listener, Brian could have been dead.

As it was, he was a whisper away from being dead. He was rushed to hospital where, for the next six weeks, all you heard from me was heavy breathing, which didn't require a great deal of acting. I was still paid the full fee, of course!

Jennifer didn't know Siobhan was in the car, but nearly losing her husband made her want to forgive him and take him back.

The affair ended with a tragi-comedy as Brian, still in hospital, but by then just about able to get out of bed, told Siobhan she had to go. 'I'm going, Brian,' she answered. Then Joe Grundy arrived and said, 'I saw Siobhan Hathaway as I was coming in. I don't know what she's doing here.' As he was talking, Brian looked out of the window and saw Siobhan walking to her car, and out of his life – it was a very poignant moment, because the listener knew that, while he was keeping up a front with Joe, Brian was crying inside. That was the last he saw of her for several years.

On the Radio 4 show *That Reminds Me*, I introduced myself as 'the man who has spent over twenty years kissing and making love to the back of his hand'. That's not quite true any more.

When Brian had his first affair, with Caroline, we recorded in mono, not stereo, and it was all rather chaste so, in that case, I did demurely kiss the back of my hand. In stereo, however, the sound is so acute that if, when required, you kiss the back of your hand and both actors are on different microphones, your lips are actually about two feet apart – and that's exactly what it sounds like. So Caroline Lennon and I had to do the kissing for real.

Mind you, if they were to give Brian an affair with an actress who resembled the back end of a bus, I might still go back to kissing the back of my hand! But Caroline is a beautiful and talented actress. Unlike the character of Siobhan, who was quite hard, Caroline was so warm and giggly and we had a great laugh playing the romantic scenes. I have to wear glasses when I read and, there we would be, both of us holding scripts in one hand, a pencil in the other and we'd have to kiss and say the lines. Her script would hit my glasses or my glasses would fall off, or she'd kiss me particularly well and they'd steam up – and so often we found it very hard not to giggle. Rarely romantic!

Caroline was such a good sport for playing the part so beautifully and enjoying the storyline ... and I'm eternally grateful for the fact that she cleaned her teeth regularly and never ate a huge garlicky meal before we had to kiss!

On my 'This is Your Life', which happened shortly after the Siobhan affair, I had Judy sitting on my right looking fantastic and Michael Aspel announced, 'Now, tonight you're here with Judy, but here to greet you is Angela Piper, who plays your wife, Jennifer Aldridge, and Caroline Lennon who plays Siobhan Hathaway, your mistress!' On they came, so I had my real wife, my fictitious wife and my mistress – I felt like some Eastern potentate for a minute, until they ruined it by saying horrid things about me. Caroline looked stunning, like a film star and, when she'd finished insulting me, I said to Michael, 'I wish she'd looked like that when we were having the affair!'

The ratings for The Archers shot up during the Siobhan storyline and that rather neatly coincided with the fiftieth year of the programme in 2001. In February, to celebrate this milestone, Prince Charles threw a party at St James's Palace and all the great and the good were there. It was awash with celebrities such as Cilla Black, Barry Norman, Stephen Fry and Martin Clunes, among many others, and a number of us were a little anxious that we, the cast, would be rather swamped by the glitterati. We needn't have worried. They were all there because of their love of *The Archers*. Whatever fame they had (and almost to a man their fame was much greater than ours), on that night they were there to celebrate fifty years of the programme. The cabaret that night was the Dead Ringers team, who all did their *Archers'* impressions, and I shall never forget Jan Raven's playing of the part of Ruth and making the entire assembled company say, 'Ooh noo!'

Another guest at the party was John Major, who asked me whether there was anything about the part of Brian that I wasn't happy with.

'Yes,' I replied. 'I am the only playing member of the MCC in the whole cast and Brian is just about the only man in the village who's never played cricket for the local team.'

Norma Major, like her husband, is a fan of *The Archers* and was once a guest at the studio, where she sat in on the read-through of an episode. One of the children wasn't present, because the child actors are often recorded and slotted in later, so Norma played the child – very well, too.

The fiftieth anniversary bash was one of the first events that Camilla Parker Bowles had attended and we heard through the grapevine that Prince Charles thought it was one of the happiest parties he'd ever had at St James's Palace. I do hope so. Funnily enough, it coincided with the frightful outbreak of foot-and-mouth disease. I couldn't help thinking of the irony that in 1951 *The Archers* had been created as a drama programme to impart countryside and agricultural information to its audience and here we were, fifty years on, doing exactly the same thing with the foot-and-mouth crisis. It's extraordinary how history repeats itself.

A few weeks later, Judy and I were part of the Farm Aid concert at the Albert Hall, and Angela Rippon introduced us to a packed house. It was an amazing feeling, walking up on stage to a huge cheer from the crowd, most of whom must have been *Archers* listeners. Afterwards, in the line-up, as Prince Charles came striding towards me, he put out his hand and said, 'We can't go on meeting like this.' 'I don't see why not,' I thought.

In October 2002, I was invited by the late Wendy Richard to attend her Variety Club of Great Britain tribute lunch at the Savoy. Held to honour her forty years in show business, Wendy was an enormous fan of *The Archers,* so I was thrilled to attend. At the time I was waiting for an operation on my hip, which was extremely painful, but I didn't want to miss out on such a delightful celebration.

During a break halfway through lunch, Wendy came over and threw her arms around me, and in my ear she whispered, 'Angela Rippon and I think you're the sexiest bastard in show business!' When you've got an aching hip, that's a wonderful thing to hear.

After the lunch, I limped in a slightly inebriated way up the Strand, got a taxi home, opened the front door, walked in and there was Judy, standing at the ironing board, with an iron in her hand.

'Darling,' I announced. 'Stop ironing. I've got something to tell you. I want you to know that at the lunch, Wendy Richard whispered in my ear, "Angela Rippon and I think you're the sexiest bastard in show business".'

And Judy just said, 'Only in show business!'

A month later, in November, Rachel Johnson, Boris's sister, rang me. At the time, Brian was at his cockiest, and still getting away with juggling those balls, and Rachel wanted to write an article about me for the *Spectator.* She asked if I would meet her for breakfast in Hampstead. I walked into the designated café at about quarter past nine and there she was. We shook hands and she went slightly red. In my experience journalists don't blush, so I was a little surprised.

'I've just got to tell you something before we start,' said Rachel. 'Before I left home, I rang my mother and I told her I was meeting Charles Collingwood, who plays Brian Aldridge, for breakfast this morning and she said, "Oh, *do* be careful, darling!"'

A couple of weeks later, I went into the King Edward VII Hospital in London for my hip operation. It was carried out by Sarah Muirhead-Allwood, who had previously replaced both the Queen Mother's hips. She told me she was going to give me a Birmingham hip, because 'it's for the younger man', which cheered me up immensely.

The op was in the evening, and when my time came the charming lady anaesthetist told me, 'I'm going to put you to sleep now.'

Apparently my last words as I drifted off were, 'Do be careful, won't you? Because five million people depend on me.' It must have been the anaesthetic!

The anaesthetist happened to be great friends with the parents of one of my daughter Jane's friends, and in fact she was having dinner with them the following evening. My daughter later told me that when she arrived, bursting with excitement, she blurted, 'You'll never guess who I put to sleep last night!'

'Who?' asked the fascinated party.

'I had Brian Aldridge lying there, and just think what he's been doing for the last year! I could have done *anything*! I had such power.'

Well, thankfully she didn't and I woke up as scheduled.

The operation was a success but I was in a certain amount of pain, as you can imagine, and to make matters worse I couldn't pee. I tried to pee but couldn't do it, so the sister told me, 'There's only thing for it; you'll have to have a catheter.'

Just imagine my feelings. I'm Brian Aldridge, the JR of Ambridge; I'm in the middle of a steamy affair; and, according to Wendy Richard, I'm the sexiest bastard in show business. And there I was with a sore hip and about to be fitted with a catheter.

Usually I'm quite brave, but I knew where this had got to go – and I was very apprehensive. There was a knock on the door and an Irish nurse appeared.

'Hello, Mr Collingwood,' she said, in her lilting accent. 'I'm afraid there's an etiquette about all this – I'm going to have to hold your penis.'

And I looked at her and said, 'Darling, if you can find it, you can hold it. It saw you come in the door and shot inside!'

A couple of days later the tube had to be taken out and a different nurse appeared. It was just coming up to Christmas, and it was about six o'clock in the morning, and she bustled in with the words, 'I have to tell you I'm your biggest fan. I absolutely love the storyline. I adore Brian.'

'And they've sent *you* to take this out?' I said. 'Are you going to tell me this *isn't* your Christmas party story?'

'I wouldn't tell a soul,' she assured me.

'Oh really!' I thought.

Having got that over with, I was dreaming of a family Christmas when my surgeon, Sarah Muirhead-Allwood, came into my room.

'Right, Charles, you have a choice,' she informed me. 'Tell me, is Brian going to stay with Jennifer, or is he going to go off with Siobhan?'

'I'm sorry,' I said, panicking. 'I can't possibly tell you. I'm sworn to secrecy.' She gave me a steely look and swanned out of the room saying, 'Well *you* won't be going home for Christmas!' I must emphasize that this was a private room and, quite apart from missing my family, I was wondering how much longer I could afford to stay there. Luckily she came back seconds later. 'You're fine,' she said, laughing. 'You can go home tomorrow.'

So off I hobbled, on crutches, to begin my recuperation.

SEVENTEEN

This is Your Life

Having been in the studio until the day before my hip operation, I wasn't due back at work for nearly three weeks, by which time I was mobile but still had to be driven everywhere by Judy. On 10 January 2003, I was still hobbling around, but we decided it was time to give our first dinner party since the op and we invited eight people, including Jane, who lived in Pimlico at the time.

That morning, my agent Natasha Stevenson was called by the BBC *This Is Your Life* team, who told her they wanted to do a programme on me and asked how they might get in touch with Judy.

'I represent his daughter as well,' said my quick-thinking agent. 'If I tell Jane, she can tell her mother, so there won't be any suspicious phone calls.'

Natasha rang Jane, who was thrilled. 'I'm seeing Mum tonight,' she said. 'I'll tell her then.'

That evening, Judy and I were pouring our guests drinks in the drawing room when Jane arrived. She walked in and could barely manage, 'Hello' before saying, 'Mummy, I've got something in my eye, can you help me? I've got something in my eye.'

Somewhat surprised, Judy said, 'Darling, you're twenty-three years of age, calm down.'

'Please, Mummy, *please.*' She was suddenly eleven again.

'Jane, I've got a lot of cooking to do and I'm entertaining our guests,' Judy muttered rather irritably. 'Just go and look in the mirror.'

But Jane was having none of it, and dragged Judy out of the room still moaning, 'I've got something in my eye.'

In the kitchen, she dropped the act and said, 'Mummy, sit down.' Judy was getting increasingly cross.

'Mummy they're doing Daddy on *This Is Your Life.*'

Apparently Judy shot out of the chair, threw both arms in the air and then did a dance with Jane, singing, 'Yes, oh yes, oh yes, oh yes.' Jane quickly told her that it had to be kept from me – because she knew her mother's instinct was to burst in on our guests and say 'Guess what everybody?' Poor Judy!

What followed were the most nerve-wracking three weeks of her life, in which she lied to me constantly. Luckily, because of my hip, I was under orders to go out for an hour's walk every day, so Judy used the time I was out of the house to make numerous phone calls and give the BBC names and addresses.

In an attempt to maintain secrecy, there was always a password for each *This Is Your Life* subject. When the production team rang anybody, they never used names, just the password – mine was 'cricket' – and family and friends were told this in advance. It was all very cloak and dagger, and all this secrecy meant that Judy went through weeks of torment.

I remember how puzzled I was that we had been invited to a number of dinner parties and they all cancelled. I began to worry and said to Judy, 'What's going on? Why is everybody pulling out of these dinner parties?'

In fact, they had all rung Judy, saying they were terrified that after two or three drinks they would let something slip.

On the day before the show Judy drove me up to Birmingham and we stayed at our usual hotel. On the morning of 29 January, she dropped me at the BBC, I got out of the car with my stick and hobbled off to the studio, and Judy drove back home to London. At last she knew she wouldn't have to see me again until we were at the *This Is Your Life* studio that night, and later she told me, 'As I dropped you off, I drove up the street, shouting, "Thank God! It's not my problem any more!"'

Sadly, two days earlier, Angela Piper's father had died, aged ninety-eight. She loved him dearly and was deeply upset when her husband called the studio, while we were recording, so I spent the next two days saying to the producer, 'She doesn't have to come up for the Wednesday recording. Let's do her scenes at a later date.'

'No, really, Charles, she wants to come,' I was told and I thought, 'Fair enough, perhaps it would help her to take her mind off it all.' That Wednesday, Angie arrived for the last episode of the day, which was due to finish at seven o'clock. We only had two scenes together, so I took the producer to one side and suggested, 'Let's do Angie's scenes first so she can go home.'

'No, no,' he said. 'I want to do both your scenes last.' 'How callous can you be?' I thought.

Those of us in that episode had been told that, on that day, there would be television cameras there to film a scene from the producers' gallery, which they did from time to time, for the BBC archives, so I didn't give them a moment's thought. I also saw various people wandering in and out the studio, but they were appointing a new producer at the time, so I assumed it was part of the interview process. Of course, when I mentioned it to the other actors they just agreed with me because they were all in on it.

Unusually, our editor Vanessa had asked me to come up to her office for a cup of tea that day. 'You've had so much to do in *The Archers* in the last year,' she explained. 'I'd really love your input into how you feel the programme is going.' Flattered, I did as I was bid and sat for the best part of an hour while Vanessa asked me various questions. Occasionally the phone would ring and she would apologize, tell the caller she was busy, and carry on. We had some tea and eventually she dismissed me with a 'Thank you, Charles, that's absolutely fascinating, I'm really grateful.'

I went away thinking, 'Well, nobody's ever asked my opinion before. I must be important.' It turned out the only reason I was in Vanessa's office was so that they could film the preamble to the show with Michael Aspel, and as long as she had me trapped in there, I wasn't going to bump into him.

Apparently, as I left Vanessa's office, Angela Piper was coming along the passage with her cocktail frock and she had to dive into a script cupboard so I wouldn't see her! I was oblivious to it all.

The strangest thing, however, was that some of the cast were hanging around. Normally, when we've finished our episodes, we are out that door like bats out of hell.

'Why are you still here?' I asked Barry Farrimond, who plays young Ed Grundy.

'I'm meeting my sister for a drink,' he said, which was fair enough.

I did notice that whenever I spoke to Richard Attlee (Kenton) he went bright red, but some people do, don't they?

We came to the last episode of the day, and Angela Piper and I were in the studio, me with my stick. Rather thoughtfully, the director, Kerry Davies, said, 'Charles, we've got the cameras filming you. Why don't you put your stick down? You don't want to be seen with a stick, I'm sure.'

So I put the stick down, did the scene and we were just about to leave for the day when Kerry caught us at the studio door and said, 'Angie, Charles, I'm so sorry, but it's such a good scene, would you mind if we just did it once more? We'd just like to bring the cameras into the studio so that they can film you both in close-up?'

The camera was set up, and the director said, 'Action' and we started replaying the scene where Brian is fighting to keep his life with Jennifer together and saying, 'Jennifer I didn't mean it ...'

'Brian, you dare look at me like that again, you think ...'

'I'm sorry, I'm sorry, darling.'

We got about a page in when, suddenly, there was a terrible commotion. I heard the studio door banging, and my first thought was, 'Oh my God! Some nutter who's got a thing about unfaithful men has got past the security and he's going to kill me!' It all happened so fast. I put my hand out behind me and felt cashmere and, I promise you, in that moment I thought, 'Nutters don't wear cashmere!' At that point I looked up and saw the iconic bright red book and Michael Aspel's face beaming above it.

'Charles Collingwood,' he was saying, 'This is your life.'

It's not often I'm lost for words, but all I could come up with was, 'What? I don't believe it! You're kidding!'

'We've got a car outside to take you to the studio, where your family are waiting to have a big party,' he continued. 'Are you happy?'

'Yes, of course,' I replied. Vanessa, the producers and all the actors who hadn't gone home were gathered round. 'But it's seven o'clock. Where are we going?'

'Teddington,' said Michael.

'Teddington!' That's over 100 miles from Birmingham.

'We start filming at quarter past ten,' explained Michael. 'Forgive me, Charles, I've got to go in the car ahead and prepare the script, so I'm off.'

The producer said she would be travelling with me and, as I

walked towards the car, with my stick, I asked, 'Can I ring Judy and tell her?' and then it dawned on me. 'Judy already knows, doesn't she?'

'I think Judy knows a little bit about this,' she laughed.

'Yes,' I thought. 'The lying cow!'

'What will I wear?' I asked.

'I'm sure you'll find that's all taken care of.'

And so we sped down the M40 across to the studios at Teddington, got there about nine o'clock, and I was taken round the back of the TV studios to the dressing room, where I found all my best clothes, suits and jackets, my favourite ties and all the things Judy knew I might want to wear. There was a TV monitor, a bowl of fruit, some sandwiches and a bottle of champagne and, I can't be sure, but I've got a feeling that as soon as I was inside, they locked the door so I couldn't escape. They don't want to risk people running away or trying to find out who else is in the building.

I sat there, trying to come to terms with the madness of it all, watching a nature programme on the TV that was full of animals shagging. 'I can't get away from infidelity,' I thought.

Eventually they were ready for me and I left my dressing room and limped, leaning on my stick, to the side of the stage, where Michael was standing with the producer.

'I don't want to have my stick now,' I said to the producer. 'How far is it from the big doors to the chair?'

'Twelve paces,' she answered.

'Michael, you won't walk too fast, will you?' I asked.

'Charles, it's your show,' he assured me. 'You walk at any pace you like.' What a gentleman.

When the music started playing and those famous doors slid open, I was overwhelmed. There was an enormous cheer; it seemed that hundreds of people had turned out at quarter past ten at night, for me. There were even people there whom I hadn't seen since school. No sooner had I sat down than I was joined by my darling (devious) Judy, along with Toby, Jane and Barney, who'd come all the way from the Sierra Nevada in Spain.

Friends and colleagues came on to say their piece, including Michael Buerk who described me as 'the last remaining true Englishman, from a gentler age, forever in a cravat!' Some were on film, including Wendy Richard, bless her heart, and Ronnie Pickup, with whom I had been at RADA.

Quite the biggest surprise was Bernard Manning. I hadn't seen him for nearly twenty years. He didn't say hello, he shuffled on, and said, 'Those see-through wigs are marvellous, Charles!'

I asked him if he was well, and he quipped, 'No, I've one pill for my heart, another pill for my diabetes, a pill for me brain, a pill for me back and a pill for me stomach. I wake up every morning, I nudge me elbow sideways and if I don't feel wood I get up.'

In 1981, during the run of *Under Manning*, the series I had done with Bernard, Judy and I had on one occasion been at the Embassy Club as his guests and, after a bottle of champagne, had been hauled up on stage to 'busk it' with Bernard for twenty minutes (not for the faint-hearted). At the end of my 'tribute' on *This Is Your Life*, Bernard said 'Thoroughly deserved, you've done really well, Charles, I'm very proud of you. You'll never make any fucking money, but ...' Which had to be edited out. Then he finished with, 'It's lovely to see your family and lovely to see Judy looking so gorgeous – better than that old slag you used to bring up to the Embassy Club!'

Judy and I cried with laughter, the whole place rocked. We knew he was poking fun at Judy, but quite a lot of my first wife's friends thought he was referring to her. Oops!

Two weeks after the broadcast, Judy and I were at a Variety Club lunch at the Grosvenor House Hotel, with 2,000 people and, between courses, I popped out for a pee. On my way to the loo, a voice behind me was calling, 'Charles! Charles!' I turned round and there was Ronnie Corbett, whom I had never met before.

'Charles,' he said. 'I just want to tell you that your *This Is Your Life* had more humour and sincerity than any I've ever seen.'

Now, he really *is* famous so that compliment was the icing on the cake for me.

Back in Brian's life, there wasn't much contact with Siobhan for a while after she nearly killed him in the road accident. She and Rauiri moved to Germany, but a couple of years later they met up quite by chance, when Brian was at an agricultural show in Paris and Siobhan was working as an interpreter there. Jennifer had come with him on the trip but, mercifully, was out shopping and never found out she was there.

We actually went to Paris to record the scenes, which was fabulous. Siobhan was with her German boyfriend Dieter and Rauiri, who was now over two and only speaking German, who wouldn't talk to or acknowledge Brian at all. The three of us had a frosty scene where Dieter dismissed Brian, and Siobhan said, 'He's nothing in my life.' But in another scene, when just the two of them had a drink together, there was still a little warmth. If you've been in love, even if you haven't seen each other for a while, you can still see what it was that first attracted you.

Brian was devastated to be separated from his little boy, although he was keeping in touch as much as possible. Jennifer allowed him to send birthday cards and presents, but Rauiri wasn't interested.

Then for Brian and Siobhan came the most dramatic twist of the lot. In 2007, Vanessa announced, 'Siobhan's going to die.' It was tough on Caroline. If you're in a programme like *The Archers* anything's better than dying! Up until that point we would occasionally hear her voice on the end of the phone, but there was always the possibility that she would come back. However, Caroline was very philosophical about it and thankful that it was a hell of a story to go out on, at least.

The writers had worked out the long-term plan from the beginning. They had Siobhan leaving Dieter and Germany, mainly because they didn't want Brian's son to reappear some time down the line only speaking German! Siobhan moved to Ireland and Rauiri was played by an Irish lad called Matthew Rockett, who they pre-recorded in Dublin, so I never actually met him. At the start, the producers thought that they would only use him a few times but he became a cult figure in Ireland and they couldn't write him out. The Irish listeners were writing in saying, 'We want more of this little boy.'

Brian spent a lot of time with Siobhan in Ireland when she was dying of terminal cancer, time that was mostly tolerated by the long-suffering Jennifer, but not always with her knowledge. Inevitably, it dragged the whole affair up again, so Jenny cried a lot and went through tremendous anguish, which, of course, made wonderful radio.

In all soaps, some stories are imposed upon the actors, and the audience don't believe them because they don't make sense for the character. The reason Siobhan's story worked was because everybody knew Brian had that wandering eye and, as many an unfaithful husband has found, there can come a time when you lose your heart. When Siobhan told Brian, 'I've got cancer, I need you to come over,' people understood why he did just that.

The final scenes with Caroline weren't easy. We all felt a responsibility to get it right, knowing there were listeners to whom this might be applicable, who had lost loved ones or maybe even had a similar illness themselves.

As Siobhan lay on her deathbed the next question was, of course, what to do with Rauiri? Her family were pretty useless, her mother was too old so there were only two options left. Determined, Brian presented Jennifer with the choice, 'This is the situation. Either he moves in to Home Farm and we bring him up together, or I'm off. I'll take him away.'

Once again, Jennifer had to go through extreme anguish as she weighed up the pros and cons; she consulted the children, she consulted her mother, and it was an appalling situation for Brian to put her in. In the end, she decided to hold onto her life with Brian, knowing that Siobhan would finally, irrevocably, be out of the picture and to cope with bringing up their little boy. It made Jennifer a much more sympathetic character. A lot of people may have thought, 'stupid woman', but the vast majority thought 'Fantastic. Lucky bloody Brian.'

In the last week of Siobhan's life, Caroline got paid for doing very little, just a few words, and in the final couple of scenes, all she did was breathe. Brian wasn't actually there when Siobhan died, he was with Rauiri in the park, and as he drove back to the house he saw the priest leaving and he knew it was too late. I had to go back and deliver a long speech to her dead body and, of course, Caroline wasn't there. All I had was a cushion to act with, because you don't have to pay a fee to a cushion.

After the storyline of the weeks before, I found it quite easy to blub so I went at the scene like a bull in a china shop, crying over her body, telling her that he'll always honour her and look after Rauiri. Rosemary Watts who, along with Julie Beckett, had directed these scenes with such sensitivity, took me to one side and said, 'Let's cut out a lot of the crying,' and later, when I heard the episode, I thought, 'you are so right'.

Rauiri moved to Home Farm and the fallout from the affair continued to rage, with Brian's daughter Alice only finding out about Rauiri when he was about to move in. She went off to university without a word and Debbie didn't speak to him for a year.

But time heals all and the Aldridges seem to have repaired the damage now. Who knows what may lurk round the corner though?

Brian may have worked his way through half the women in Borsetshire but, maddeningly, he's never tried it on with Shula! Probably just as well because an on-air romance between a real-life husband and wife might be one step too far for the listener. I suspect Judy's secretly delighted – she gets kissed by me enough at home, without having to put up with it at work as well!

EIGHTEEN

Retrospective

On a recent trip to a supermarket, on a particularly wet afternoon, I was wearing my Barbour, my cap and my wellies and I was studying a selection of dental floss, my mind miles away from Ambridge. That was until I heard a woman's voice as she pushed her trolley past me, saying, out of the corner of her mouth, 'You're looking very "Brian" this morning.' I suppose I was.

On another shopping trip, I heard a mother saying to her son, who she was about to drop off at home before going on somewhere else, 'Now promise me you'll record *The Archers* at seven o'clock!'

'Yes, Mummy, I will,' he said, and I interrupted with, 'And you won't forget will you?' The mother gave a squeal because she instantly recognized the voice.

Over the years, Judy and I have been to many dinner parties where, inevitably, we are asked about *The Archers*, and normally we are asked the same questions every time. It's totally understandable. If I talk to a famous cricketer, I'm probably going to ask him the question he's been asked 500 times, because it will be the one thing that everyone wants to know. We never mind because it's flattering to be asked. There are occasions, though, when people proudly pronounce that they 'never watch *The Archers*'. You don't get too many questions about Ambridge then.

By and large, the public are very discerning and charming.

Judy and I have often been asked to open fetes and many years ago, we were at a fete in Devon when one of the villagers made a particularly personal remark to Judy. She had, in a very beautiful, distinguished way, gone prematurely grey, and this woman came up and said, 'Oh, you're Shula. I never thought Shula would have *grey* hair.' She went for the bottle shortly after that – the blond bottle, not the alcoholic variety.

Throughout my life I have been very fortunate. Judy and I recently dined in the State Room at Buckingham Palace. Richard Stilgoe runs a charity called The Orpheus Trust, for people with learning difficulties. Prince Edward, patron of the charity, hosted a fund-raising dinner for about eighty of us. As we sat down for dinner in Buckingham Palace, Ronnie Corbett said, 'All I can say is that this is where I want to be if I'm ever under house arrest!'

I'm often asked what the secret of *The Archers* is. Apart from the script and the acting, I think it's also the signature tune and the length of the episodes. Everybody knows the tune, and it has the right feel to it. With regards to the length, fifteen minutes is perfect. So many people manage to listen to it on their journey home in the car after work, or in the kitchen preparing supper, or maybe they listen at lunchtime so it doesn't interfere with their day, and there's always the omnibus on Sunday. Nowadays, it can even be downloaded and listened to in all sorts of ways.

Over and above all that, I think *The Archers* has the right pace: it isn't too frantic, and that makes it true to life. On television you rarely see a scene when two characters simply sit down and talk reflectively about the family without moving the storyline along. We can have scenes where Phil and Jill might just be sitting at the table and talking about the children, and that's what happens in real life. And because we don't have to learn the script, our scenes, when necessary, can be longer. TV soap stars have to learn their lines, so to watch a scene longer than two minutes is quite rare, but we sometimes have scenes that last nine or ten minutes, because we just read it.

The pace of the show mirrors village life. When I was a boy living in Hampshire, I was away at boarding school for three months each time, and would come back in the holidays, get on my bicycle to go fishing or down to the shop. When I passed the postman he didn't say, 'My God, where have you been all this time?' He just said, 'Morning, Charlie.'

A number of people have told me, 'We were away for six months and we came back, turned on *The Archers* and it was just as it had been when we left.' And life's a bit like that. You can pick up where you left off and, on the whole, it isn't over-dramatic and neither should *The Archers* be.

In writing this book it just hasn't been possible, or indeed practical, to mention every single member of the cast and crew. It isn't that sort of book anyway. Suffice it to say that as one challenging storyline follows another, I'm proud to listen to my peers more than rise to the challenge. But actors always concede that they are 'only as good as the script'. How true. By far the greatest improvement overall during my time has been the quality of the writing. What a team we have. How they churn out twenty-four episodes a month, of such quality, is beyond me. Fantastic!

The team we have running the office now are 'simply the best' and are much appreciated. As for our team of studio managers and technicians – how any of them know how all those panels and knobs work is beyond me. I'm knob dyslexic, if you'll pardon the expression.

The show has now been running every week for nearly sixty

years, but the future is unknown. Recently, I have become increasingly concerned that many of those in managerial positions in the BBC come more and more from a news background and the world of journalism, and have little understanding and feeling for the world of art and music. What worries me sometimes is that the powers that be will stop giving these programmes the respect and prominence they deserve.

Not long ago I met an actor whom I had worked with in the theatre in the 1960s. I hadn't seen him for decades, so we went and had lunch.

As we ate he asked, 'How many times a week do you curse the fact that you've spent such a large part of your life playing Brian in *The Archers*?'

'Curse?' I said. 'What do you mean?'

'Oh, Charles, come on,' he said. 'Think of all those wonderful parts you could have played at the National Theatre or the RSC. You're a good actor.'

'Thank you,' I said. 'But I didn't see the contracts. Which parts were they that floated past you with my name on?'

OK, in an ideal world there would have been times when I would love to have done other things, and maybe *The Archers* has stopped me doing some of them, but to create a character like Brian Aldridge and play him for over half of my life, to an audience of five million; to have the feedback and the reactions, particularly with the Siobhan story and the affair – well, that'll do for me. I'm sure when I was at RADA I didn't think, 'I know, I'm going to do two years here and then go and spend forty years playing a character on radio,' but I have no complaints.

In fact, it has been and is an enormous privilege to play the part of Brian Aldridge in the longest-running soap opera in the world. In this day and age, when television screens dominate, we have the most discerning, intelligent, wonderful audience and for that I am extremely grateful.

Epilogue

As I said, Richard Stilgoe wrote us the most wonderful opening for our show *Laughter and Intrigue,* a poem in rhyming couplets, incorporating us as Charles and Judy and the characters we play in *The Archers.* It got us off to a great start every time we performed our show.

In 2001, Judy and I celebrated our silver wedding anniversary and, being a member of the MCC, I hired the museum at Lord's, where we invited 170 friends to a party. I asked Richard if he'd be kind enough to just say a few words and, as always, he entertained our guests royally. He finished by reading the poem that he'd written for us in the show, but had adapted specially for that night. I would like to share this masterpiece with you all.

Charles and Judy

Charles and Judy are both actors, an honourable profession,
A glorious vocation, a magnificent obsession.
Which begins with dreams of Hamlet, Desdemona, Lear, Camille,
As you sit at home and listen for the telephone to peal.
Twelve months later you reflect upon the actors' bitter pill,
You've died in *Holby City*, been run over in *The Bill*.
Played a very junior midwife in the series they aborted,
And said one word in *EastEnders* which predictably was 'Sorted!'
So imagine their relief when over coffee and focaccia,
William Smethurst said 'We'd like you each to be an Archer.'
They're no longer Charles and Judy, one is Shula, one is Brian,

And Vanessa Whitburn rules them with a rod of purest iron.
For fifteen minutes every night, while sheep and heifers munch,
Their lives are carved and served up, then repeated after lunch.
And every Sunday morning in between the toast and roast,
They regurgitate the pieces that upset us all the most.
It took them by surprise at first that someone had the power,
To take them over daily for a quarter of an hour.
To turn Charles into somebody obsessed with stags and sex,
While Judy married Mark, who sadly died of sound effects.
For nothing helps the ratings like a sudden ghastly death,
So when a batch of scripts arrive you read with bated breath.
'How are you, Brian?' said Jennifer, 'Thank God, it says I'm fine,'
'But have you checked the slashing knife on your new combine?'
For people seldom realize that all the Ambridge greenery,
Is liberally scattered with lethal farm machinery.
You can leap from burning buildings and emerge with only
    bruises,
But when an actor meets a tractor, the actor always loses.
It's frightening being an Archer, for someone writes your life,
Writes your husband, writes your children, writes your nightmare
    of a wife.
So Brian toyed with Caroline, a snobby pheasant plucker,
Then slummed with what Madonna would have called a mother
    tucker.
And now once more he's hung-ry, forget the aftermath – away,
To Brussels to eat mussels and leap on Siobhan Hathaway.
But soon 'twill be 'Siobhan, shove off, I'm finding you a bore,
I rather fancy Ruth,' but sadly Ruth replied 'Aw naw'.
Meanwhile Shula's in the vet's arms, trying to think 'Wow!'
While aware one arm two hours ago was three feet up a cow.
No wonder they take refuge with each other in real life,
It's not quite so exhausting just playing man and wife.

They've got to twenty-five now and wouldn't it be nifty,
If unlike Ramprakrash they went on to make it fifty!
So raise your glasses one and all, you must know where I'm
    heading,
To Charles and Judy, all our love, on this your silver wedding.

INDEX

(the initials CC and JB denote Charles Collingwood and Judy Bennett)